KU-501-147

HOW THE EBOOKS WORK

The eBooks are provided in EPUB file format. Please note that you will need an eBook reader installed on your device to open the file. Many devices come with this as standard, but you may still need to install one manually from Google Play.

The eBook content is identical to the content in the printed guide.

HOW TO DOWNLOAD THE WALKING EYE APP

1. Download the Walking Eye App from the App Store or Google Play.
2. Open the app and select the scanning function from the main menu.
3. Scan the QR code on this page – you will then be asked a security question to verify ownership of the book.
4. Once this has been verified, you will see your eBook in the purchased ebook section, where you will be able to download it.

Other destination apps and eBooks are available for purchase separately or are free with the purchase of the Insight Guide book.

Kingston upon Thames Libraries

KT 2305161 2	
Askews & Holts	26-Apr-2017
915.49 TRG	£8.99
HK	KT00002138

INSIGHT ⊙ GUIDES

EXPLORE

SRI LANKA

KINGSTON LIBRARIES

WITHDRAWN

KT 2305161 2

◉ Walking Eye App

Your guide now includes a free eBook to your chosen destination, for the same great price as before. Simply download the Walking Eye App from the App Store or Google Play to access your free eBook.

HOW THE WALKING EYE APP WORKS

Through the Walking Eye App, you can purchase a range of eBooks and destination content. However, when you buy this book, you can download the corresponding eBook for free. Just see below in the grey panel where to find your free content and then scan the QR code at the bottom of this page.

Destinations: Download essential destination content featuring recommended sights and attractions, restaurants, hotels and an A–Z of practical information, all available for purchase.

Ships: Interested in ship reviews? Find independent reviews of river and ocean ships in this section, all available for purchase.

eBooks: You can download your free accompanying digital version of this guide here. You will also find a whole range of other eBooks, all available for purchase.

Free access to travel-related blog articles about different destinations, updated on a daily basis.

CONTENTS

ANCIENT TEMPLES

Marvel at cave temples and ruins of ancient shrines (route 9), pay homage at the medieval Temple of the Tooth (route 6) or visit artistically restored temples in Colombo (route 2).

RECOMMENDED ROUTES FOR...

ANIMAL LOVERS

Watch the magnificent Gathering of the Elephants at Minneriya (route 10), go searching for elusive leopards in Yala (route 12) or get up close to myriad colourful creatures in Colombo's spacious zoo (route 4).

BEACHES

Laze on Negombo's sandy seafront (route 5), promenade on Mount Lavinia's golden strand (route 4) or head to Unawatuna, Sri Lanka's most popular backpacker resort with a charming cove and a laidback atmosphere (route 11).

BOTANICAL GARDENS

Get back to nature at Sri Lanka's very different botanical gardens (route 6 and route 7) and dry-zone arboretum, where you can meander along the trails under ghostly tropical trees (route 9).

COLONIAL ARCHITECTURE

Discover ornate British colonial buildings in Colombo Fort and inspiring Dutch designs in Pettah (walk 1), or a time-warp amalgamation of both in Galle Fort (tour 11).

HOTTEST CURRIES

If hotel food is too bland, search for spicier cuisine in rest houses, or in the cities of Kandy (route 6) and Colombo (route 2), where you'll find a wide spread of restaurants.

MOUNTAIN VIEWS

Peer through Ella Gap for fabulous views down to the south coast (route 8), glimpse Mount Pidurutalagala, Sri Lanka's highest peak, from Nuwara Eliya (route 7); or scramble up to Lipton's Seat (route 8) for breathtaking vistas.

TEA TREKKING

Trek through tea gardens to your heart's content at Kandapola (route 7) and Haputale (route 8), relishing the cool mountain air, then warm up with a cup of pure Ceylon tea in a plantation bungalow.

INTRODUCTION

An introduction to Sri Lanka's geography, customs and culture, plus illuminating background information on cuisine, history and what to do when you're there.

Tea plantations near Ella

EXPLORE SRI LANKA

Sri Lanka is one of Asia's ultimate island paradises, with endless miles of golden beaches and verdant tropical landscapes. But the island also boasts remarkable physical, cultural and ethnic diversity, as well as a long and dramatic history.

The shape of Sri Lanka on the map has been compared to many things: a teardrop falling from the tip of India, a pearl, a mango and (to Dutch colonists) a leg of ham. Tears were for many years the island's dominant emotion, the result of 26 years of devastating civil war which blighted the island's recent history. Since the conclusion of hostilities in 2009, however, Sri Lanka has boomed, enjoying its new-found peace and emerging once again as one of the pearls of the Indian Ocean. Indeed, this new tourism star has never burned more brightly, with large annual increases in the number of visitors to the country (up to nearly 1.8 million tourists in 2015, 17.8 percent up on the previous year, continuing a trend since 2010). And it's no surprise – Sri Lanka has everything visitors could want from a tropical holiday: beaches, culture, natural splendors, unique attractions, wildlife and more.

GEOGRAPHY AND LAYOUT

Sri Lanka is a small country: a modest 435km (271 miles) from top to bottom, and 240km (149 miles) from east to west. Lying a few degrees north of the Equator in the balmy waters of the Indian Ocean, the island has an incredibly diverse range of landscapes, from the sultry tropical beaches, coconut plantations and lowland jungles of the coast to the cool green hill country with its mist-shrouded mountains, crashing waterfalls and endless tea plantations.

Exploring the country

The island's relatively small size and recently upgraded main highways make it easy to travel between its best sights within the space of a few days. The starting point for most visitors is the commercial capital, Colombo (routes 1 and 2), easily explored either on foot or by hiring one of the motorised rickshaws (tuk-tuks) which can be seen everywhere across the island. There are also various rewarding day-trips from Colombo, into the surrounding countryside (routes 3–5), or you could make an overnight trip up to Sri Lanka's cultural capital, Kandy (route 6).

With a few more days spare you could drive north from Kandy to the ancient ruined cities and great Buddhist monuments of the Cultural Triangle (routes 9 and 10). Alternatively, head south from

New Kathiresan Kovil Temple

A traditional vessel off Unawatuna Beach

Kandy to explore the verdant tea plantations, spectacular scenery and engaging old colonial mementoes of the island's breezy hill country (tours 7 and 8) and then continue on to Yala National Park (route 12) in the south before returning to Colombo via Galle (route 11).

Many visitors will stay on Sri Lanka's west coast if they want to spend some time on the beach; resort areas include Bentota, Hikkaduwa and Ahungalla. While this area is lighter on sights than elsewhere, the miles of golden, sun-kissed beaches, tourist-oriented development and range of places to stay (see page 90) make this a hugely popular choice for sun-starved European visitors, whether for a two-week package holiday or for some R'n'R as part of a tour of the country. These beach resorts are easily reached from Colombo or Galle.

Painting a wall at the Gangaramaya Temple, Colombo

HISTORY

The first humans to arrive were the aboriginal Veddhas, who walked across from India around 16,000 BC. Around the 4th century BC, immigrants from North India began to arrive, becoming ancestors of the modern Sinhalese.

Early development of the island was mainly in the northern half, where the ancient ruins of Anuradhapura and Polonnaruwa testify to a glorious Buddhist culture and pioneering agricultural development, including the creation of huge reservoirs (tanks) and a staggeringly elaborate network of waterways and irrigation works.

After the 13th century, the island became politically fragmented, with the inland Kingdom of Kandy vying for power with a series of smaller statelettes in the south. The 16th century also saw the arrival of the Portuguese, ushering in the long colonial period during which the island would change hands between no less than three European powers.

The Portuguese gradually seized control of most of the island – apart from the remote, inland Kingdom of Kandy – before losing the island to the Dutch in 1656. The Dutch made fortunes trading on the island's spices, cinnamon, elephants and precious gemstones before being displaced at the start of the 19th century by the British, who gave the island the railways, roads, tea plantations and parliamentary democracy which survive largely unchanged to this day.

Worshippers at Sri Maha Bodhi, sacred to Buddhists

Independence finally arrived in 1948, although Sri Lanka's post-colonial history was shaped by violent tensions between the island's majority Sinahalese and minority Tamil populations, leading to a bloody 26-year civil war which raged from 1983 to 2009 between government forces and the rebel LTTE (Liberation Tigers of Tamil Eelam – or Tamil Tigers, as they're usually called). Many lives were also lost in 2004, when Sri Lanka was hit by the catastrophic Asian tsunami.

The new era of post-war peace has presented fresh political and financial challenges, although a booming economy, a resurgent tourist industry and a merciful absence of war and natural catastrophe mean that the island is finally able to look once more to the future with renewed – if cautious – optimism.

Winds of fortune

The trade winds, on which the monsoons are carried to Sri Lanka, not only keep the island watered, but also helped make it rich. In former centuries the winds provided a reliable shuttle service for traders from Greece, China, Arabia and Rome, sailing in search of spices and gems. Since these seafaring merchants had to wait for the winds to change direction before they could sail home, many decided to stay and set up business instead, developing the island's trade.

CLIMATE

The island's climate is so diverse it's possible to travel in just a few hours from the tropical heat of the coast to the cool and misty uplands of the hill country – to start the day sweating and end it shivering. There are two separate monsoon seasons, one in the northeast, the other in the southwest – from October to April, the climate is kindest in the southwest, while there is less rain in the northeast from May to October. Expect high humidity and temperatures on the coast of around 27°C (81°F). Kandy, at 305m (1,000ft), averages 20°C (68°F), and Nuwara Eliya, at 1,890m (6,200ft), just 16°C (61°F).

POPULATION

While Sri Lanka's racial diversity has caused much strife, it compensates with a diversity of culture and mutual respect between the different races despite the long-raging civil war. Interracial rivalry is fought out with games of 'we got here first', with both the Sinhalese and the Tamils arguing about precedence. The British colonial period brought about the introduction of English as a link language between the Tamils and the Sinhalese, but this link was lost when S.W.R.D Bandaranaike made Sinhala the official language. Tamils found their aspirations thwarted unless they learned Sinhala.

Around three-quarters of the island's population is Sinhalese Buddhist. The Sinhalese migrated to Sri Lanka from

Street life in Batticaloa

North India around the 4th century BC. The Tamils are Sri Lanka's second-largest ethnic group, comprising around 18 percent of the population. They claim that their Dravidian ancestors got to the island even earlier. Some five percent of the Tamil population are descendants of immigrants brought by the British for plantation labour. Most Sri Lankan Tamils are Hindus, although there are also many Tamil Christians.

Sri Lanka's Muslims have been living on the island for over a millennium, having arrived as merchants, and now mostly live on the east coast. One of the island's smallest but most colourful ethnic groups

---

DON'T LEAVE SRI LANKA WITHOUT...

Climbing to the top of Sigiriya. Ascending this unforgettable rock-fortress, one of Sri Lanka's most dramatic natural sights, gives you incredible views over the surrounding plains. See page 71.

Hitting the beach. Sri Lanka's coast is fringed with sun-soaked golden beaches and luscious palm trees; if you're short for time, head to Negombo, just half an hour from Colombo airport. See page 46.

Paying homage to the tooth. Time your visit to Kandy's Temple of the Tooth right and you'll be rewarded with a glimpse of the golden casket containing the Buddha's Tooth Relic, at this most important of pilgrimage sites in Sri Lanka. See page 51.

Sampling hoppers. A Sri Lankan breakfast staple, also found at most street cafés, these delicate little bowl-shaped pancakes are great on their own, eaten with curry or cooked with an egg in the centre. See page 17.

Catching a Kandyan dance show. Spectacularly costumed dancers perform acrobatic choreography to an insistent accompaniment of high-octane drumming. See page 51.

Visiting a tea plantation. Travel past spectacular waterfalls, verdant hills lined with tea terraces and roadside fruit sellers to reach Sri Lanka's working tea plantations, where you can have a brew and learn all about the process from plant to cup. See page 56.

Catching a cricket match. Join the crowds at a test or one-day match for an insight into Sri Lanka's other major religion: cricket. See page 24.

Taking in the view at Ella Gap. The staggering view from Ella Gap, in a charming hill country village, takes in miles of peaks, valleys and – on a clear day – the southern plateau all the way to the coast. See page 64.

Learning about Ayurveda. Ayurvedic wellness centres are found everywhere and even if you're not looking for a specific cure, the natural science behind it is fascinating to discover. See page 25.

Spotting leopards. Tracking down this elusive big cat at Yala National Park is an experience even if you don't manage a sighting, with elephants, wild boar and more to keep you diverted. See page 85.

Drummers guard Sri Maha Bodhi

is the Burghers – white, English-speaking Sri Lankans descended from European settlers, mainly Dutch and Portuguese.

The population is mainly rural (about 80 percent), although since vast tracks of mountainous jungle and arid plains are largely uninhabited, the population density is high in settled areas around the coast, and particularly in the major cities.

LOCAL CUSTOMS

Sri Lankans are a very friendly and helpful people, and will often ask you where you are from. However, beware of touts who make a living out of preying on tourists. In the evening it is the custom for Sri Lankans to have a drink together before eating quite late; people generally go home immediately after the meal rather than stay on for more drinks.

People generally are not camera shy, but if you want to take a photograph, always ask first. Sometimes they will request a copy.

Sri Lankans will forgive many breaches of etiquette, such as your eating habits (see page 107). However, when entering temples, remove your shoes and headgear as a sign of respect. Remember to be sensitive to local religious and cultural customs.

POLITICS

Sri Lanka is a parliamentary democracy with an elected executive president. The 225 members of parliament are elected separately through a complicated proportional voting system. The 2015 election, regarded as the most significant one for decades, ended the long-running dynastic rule of the Rajapakse family. The newly elected president, Maithripala Sirisena, has pledged to bring in constitutional reforms to reduce the power of the president and return the country to a parliamentary system with a Prime Minister as its leader.

Economics

The top foreign-exchange earners are the manufacture of garments exported to the West and inward remittances from Sri Lankans working overseas, mainly in the Gulf. Tourism comes third, although it is increasingly important. Agriculture (especially tea exporting) has lost its relative importance to the Sri Lankan economy, employing around 31 percent of the working population but accounting for just 7.9 percent of GDP.

The service sector is the largest component of GDP, at 56.6 percent in 2015. Industry accounts for 26.2 percent of GDP, with manufacturing of food, beverages and tobacco the largest subsector.

The per capita income of the almost 22 million inhabitants stood at US$3,637 in 2015. The people of Sri Lanka enjoy free education and healthcare, and a literacy rate of 92 percent – one of the highest in Asia and the highest in South Asia. Since the end of the war in 2009, the nation has hoped it is time for its full potential to be realised.

Travelling by tuk–tuk

Women working in the tea plantations

Travel visa. Visitors to Sri Lanka should obtain an Electronic Travel Authorisation (ETA) before they travel (www.eta.gov.lk/slvisa). This allows tourist entry for up to 30 days, for US$30. Visas can be extended to three months at the Immigration Service Centre in Colombo. Fees vary depending on what country you are a national of. Visitors from Singapore, the Seychelles and the Maldives are exempt from needing a visa.

Staying healthy. The risk of malaria is increasingly minimal in most areas that tend to be visited by tourists, but be sure to ask your doctor for the latest advice. If you are advised to take prophylaxis, you may need to start a course of medication up to a fortnight before you leave for your trip. There is, however, a risk of dengue fever.

Sun and heat. Sunburn and even sunstroke are a risk in lowland Sri Lanka, whether you're lying on the beach or exploring ancient monuments. An umbrella is never out of place, both for warding off rain and sheltering from the sun.

Giving gifts. If you are lucky enough to be invited to a local home, a present of a box of biscuits or even something you've brought with you from overseas, like a souvenir ornament or duty-free chocolate, would be appreciated.

Tuk-tuk touting. The drivers of motorised rickshaws, called tuk-tuks, can't bear to see a foreigner walking; you'll need to be firm in refusing them.

Road sense. Many of Colombo's streets have been changed from dual traffic to one-way, and some roads are closed occasionally, so be patient when you discover you have to negotiate an unexpected diversion.

Safe swimming. Swimming from Mount Lavinia Beach (see route 4) is safe and very popular, but make sure someone you know guards your belongings, otherwise you might not have any when you return from the sea. Note that there are places where swimming can be dangerous because of riptides.

Take the train. An intercity express train with seats that can be booked in advance leaves Colombo Fort station at about 7am every morning and arrives in Kandy at 9.45am. The return express leaves Kandy at 3pm and arrives in Colombo at 5.35pm, in time for dinner.

Nature reserve. Even if Adisham isn't open, the Tangamalai Nature Reserve (open access; free) directly beyond it is worth visiting, protecting a beautiful area of tropical forest, it is home to a rich array of bird life, with lots of monkeys too.

Park formalities. To visit Yala National Park, you will have to hire a jeep and a tracker, as well as pay an admission fee per person and per vehicle. Jeep safaris cost less the nearer you stay to the park. Be prepared for a long wait at the visitor centre as entrance fees are calculated and your passport details laboriously copied into a ledger by hand; no passport, no entry.

A traditional Sri Lankan breakfast

FOOD AND DRINK

Sri Lankan cuisine may not be renowned beyond the island's shores, but it features a distinctive and delicious blend of flavours based on local ingredients and spices, from the heat of chillies to the sweetness of coconuts.

Far more than a variation on the classic cuisines of neighbouring India, Sri Lankan cooking has its own unique set of flavours, inspired by the island's abundant natural produce and the huge variety of spices grown here. Rice and curry remains culinary king, but with fiercer flavours than in India and with sauces based on coconut milk and fiery chilli sambols, making it somewhere between Indian and Thai cooking in style.

Over the centuries, Sri Lanka's visitors and invaders have contributed Indian, Chinese, Malay and Arab influences, as well as Portuguese, Dutch and British dishes. In hotel buffets you might encounter all of them at the same time, so take the chance to sample what Sri Lanka can offer – rare spices, unusual vegetables, tropical fruits and some of the world's fattest prawns, not to mention the classic Sri Lankan rice and curry, a miniature banquet all on its own.

LOCAL CUISINE

Sri Lankan food has a reputation for being deliciously hot, thanks to the use of generous quantities of chillies and other warming spices. Sri Lankan cooks don't reach for a packet of curry powder; they spend hours grinding selected spices to create a dish that is rich in flavour as well as pungent – a good cook can spend hours preparing an authentic curry. While Sri Lankans have been raised to expect their curries to be hot, visitors may be served milder versions, tamed by the addition of coconut milk.

The method of preparation has evolved over the centuries, with a dash of influence by Portuguese settlers in the 16th century. The abundance of fresh vegetables (some introduced by the British in the 19th century) and forest roots, as well as locally grown spices like cardamom, cinnamon, cloves and curry leaves – known as *karapincha* in Sinhala – contribute to making Sri Lankan curries special. This small green leaf adds a distinctive flavour with an aroma akin to lime and sesame when crushed, and also has the reputation of being good for lowering cholesterol.

Curries are flavoured with different spices to match the main ingredient. Meat or fish, and vegetables like eggplant, cabbage, beans and even pine-

Colourful ingredients that pack a punch

apple, lend themselves to hot curries. Root vegetables and cashew nuts work better as mild curries. Curries cooked in the traditional way – in a clay pot over a wood fire – take on more spicy flavour, thanks to the time taken to cook them.

Rice is the staple, and there are over 15 varieties in Sri Lanka. A favourite is the red country rice, *kakuluhaal*. This strain is full of vitamins and has a nutty flavour, as the grains are left unpolished. White rice, whether the ball-shaped *sambha*, the long-grained *basmati* or the white *milchard*, is widely available.

Rice and curry meals, served at the table in bowls or on buffets, always have the meat or fish curries cooked and served separately from the vegetable curries, so vegetarians can select what to eat without qualms.

BREAKFAST

Appa (hoppers), a type of pancake with crispy edges and made of rice flour or plain flour with coconut milk and yeast, is a favourite Sri Lankan breakfast dish. It can also be served with a fried egg nestling in it and is sensational when eaten with a beef curry and *seeni sambol*, a sweet, spicy onion relish.

Kiribath (milk rice) is a breakfast dish made with rice, cooked in coconut cream or fresh milk and spices. This is considered an auspicious meal and is eaten during special occasions – on the first of each month, or when welcoming visitors.

LUNCH

Lunch packets of rice and curry (usually rice with three vegetable curries and one meat curry) are the mainstay of office workers. Packets are available in simple cafés and from street stalls throughout Colombo. When Sri Lankans are touring the country, they typically lunch in rest houses where a typical spread would consist of curries made of plantain blossoms, radishes, lentils, beef, fish, beans and eggplant, accompanied by bitter *gourd sambol* (a relish), *gotakola medun* (a leaf salad), devilled potatoes, a spicy mango chutney, and papadum served with fried red chillies and chunks of dry fish.

You won't go short of rice and curry

String hoppers

DINNER

For dinner at home, a Sri Lankan might have a curry served with *indiappa* (string hoppers), a Sri Lankan invention that resembles fine noodles. It is made by squeezing a mixture of rice flour (or plain flour) and water through a colander onto bamboo trays and then steam-cooking the mix until it's fluffy.

String-hopper *biriyani* – a lunch or dinner delicacy – is produced by breaking *indiappa* into small pieces and then cooking it with spices, meat and cashew nuts. *Lamprais* is a Dutch variation in which rice and curries are wrapped in banana leaves and steamed with chicken or beef.

OTHER DELICACIES

Old Dutch and Portuguese delicacies such as *bolo fiado* (laminated cake) and *boroa* (semolina biscuits) are another element of Sri Lankan cuisine. Biriyani, a traditional Muslim rice-and-meat dish, and Tamil *thosai* (pancakes) and *vade* (fritters), have also become part of local cooking. *Pittu* is ground rice or plain flour mixed with coconut and then steam-cooked in a bamboo container; it is eaten with coconut milk, or with meat or fish.

A kind of flimsy pancake, *godamba roti* is a particular favourite among Muslims. It is fascinating to see this being made: with each turn of the expert handler's wrist, a small ball of flour becomes

longer and flatter. Another popular dish is *watallappan*, a deliciously rich dessert concocted out of *jaggery* (a coarse brown sugar made from the sap of the date palm), eggs, milk and cashew nuts.

SNACKS

Local snacks, known as 'short eats', consist of savoury bite-sized pastries or rolls which can be bought in pastry shops to eat in or take away. There are many types, including miniature loaves baked and stuffed with *seeni sambol*, fried pancakes with a beef, fish, chicken or vegetable filling, meat or chicken patties, and 'cutlets', deep-fried soft round balls of mashed tuna.

FRUIT

The island's cornucopia of tropical fruits includes pineapple, passion fruit, pomegranate, papaya, avocados, mangoes, several kinds of guava, more than a dozen varieties of banana (including the much-loved sweet red bananas), and many more exotic offerings that will not be familiar from back home. Look out for the deep purple, delicately grape-flavoured mangosteen, star apples and the maverick *durian*, a huge green fruit whose pungent smell usually puts people off sampling its delicious, nougat-flavoured flesh. Even bigger than the durian is the *jak*, the world's largest fruit, which is eaten both raw and in cooked in curries.

Sweet hoppers

Preparing a king coconut for drinking

WHERE TO EAT

Eating in the restaurant of your hotel or guesthouse is generally a safe bet: food turnover is usually high, as are standards of freshness and hygiene. That's where you will also be able to get non-spicy dishes like grilled fish or barbecued lobster. There will always be a choice, so you don't have to be like a Sri Lankan and have curry for every meal. Many of the island's numerous private villas and small boutique hotels also dish up superb food, although this is sometimes served only to in-house guests. The best restaurants for fusion, ethnic or continental fine dining are in Colombo. Some hotels away from the city also have good restaurants, which offer a break from stereotypical buffet food.

Village restaurants and eateries may prove testing due to the spicy food and suspect hygiene. Unlike other Asian countries, Sri Lanka has no tradition of street food. Rest houses are usually a safe bet for local food as they are used to catering for foreign travellers as well as for their usual clientele of lawyers, government officials and sales reps. A nice custom is for drivers of guests to eat free with the staff, so don't worry about inviting your chauffeur to join you for lunch.

DRINKS

All imported beverages (wines, spirits and beers) carry a high tax, making them relatively expensive. Wine is readily available, including Australian, Chilean and South African vintages. Several locally brewed beers like Lion Lager and Three Coins, are worth trying. For a taste of an authentic Sri Lankan product, try *arrack*, a feisty spirit, a bit like rum in both taste and strength, made from toddy (the sap of the coconut palm tree). Fresh, unfermented toddy is also much enjoyed by Sri Lankans, though its strong, sweaty aroma can be off-putting.

The sale of alcohol is prohibited on *Poya* (full moon) days, even to tourists staying in hotels, and on other days according to government decree. Buy your supplies the day before.

For teetotallers, there is tea, of course, as well as fruit juices, with fresh lime and soda being especially refreshing. A *thambili* (young coconut) cut open by a roadside vendor so you can drink the water within is a healthy natural beverage. Another local speciality is ginger beer made with real ginger (but make sure it's the Elephant House brand for that distinctive taste).

Food and drink prices

Throughout this book, the below is a price guide for a meal for one:

$$$$ = over Rs3000
$$$ = Rs1500–3000
$$ = Rs750–1500
$ = below Rs750

Batik design is an intricate process

SHOPPING

For many visitors, shopping is defined by what's available in their hotel gift shops – yet venturing out to nearby villages or making a point of shopping in Colombo or Kandy can yield more than batik sarongs and garish masks.

Sri Lanka's rich artistic traditions rival those of pretty much anywhere in the world. If you're prepared to shop around, there are excellent crafts to be found, and prices remain among the cheapest in Asia – although equally many of the crafts available are of shoddy quality. Alternatively, tea and spices also make excellent souvenirs.

WHAT TO BUY

In Colombo, there are plenty of superior shops – such as Odel for fashions, Paradise Road for knick-knacks and Barefoot for bright fabrics – and shopping malls like Majestic City and the upmarket Crescat (see route 2). The other main places to buy are Kandy, which has a deluge of craft shops, and Galle, famous for its gems, jewellery, lace and Dutch antiques, and now also home to a number of designer boutiques.

Local supermarkets such as the islandwide Cargills chain offer another good – if not particularly exotic – hunting ground for shoppers, usually carrying a good stock of local tea, spices and other local edibles at far cheaper prices than you'll find in hotel gift shops and the like.

Bargaining is the order of the day in smaller shops. A request for a 'small discount' or a 'special price' can sometimes work, especially if you're making a big purchase or buying several items.

Gems

An immense assortment of gems are to be found, with blue sapphires being the best buy. Gleaming star sapphires and star rubies are beautiful when set as rings and pendants. Alexandrites are olive-green in natural light, turning a raspberry red under artificial light. Cat's Eye, so called because it has a streak of light in the middle like the eye of a cat, comes in hues of honey-yellow and apple-green. Other popular stones are amethysts, garnets, aquamarines and moonstones.

Only buy in quality shops such as those in five-star hotels. You might find cheaper prices out of Colombo. For example, in Bentota, Aida Gems and Jewellery (12A Mangala Mawatha, Bentota; www.aidasrilanka.com) has a solid reputation. Locally crafted, highly

Woodcarvings

Gems galore

fashionable costume jewellery of exquisite design can be purchased at Stone 'n' String, which has Colombo outlets in Majestic City, the World Trade Centre and Crescat, and a branch in Kandy inside Kandy City Centre.

Batiks

Colourful batik designs involving motifs of elephants, peacocks and Kandyan dancers make attractive sarongs, tablecloths and wall hangings. Laksala, the government handicraft shop with branches in Colombo, Kandy and Galle, stock them, as do many other crafts shops.

Handicrafts

Craft shops stock an extensive range of items like mats, masks, drums, coconut-shell dolls, porcupine-quill boxes, lace, reed, basket and bamboo-ware, lacquerware, wooden figurines, shell crafts, and silver and brassware. The varied representations of Sri Lanka's elephants, painted batik-style or carved from ebony, are attractive.

Several Colombo shops sell unique items such as cushion covers inlaid with the Sinhala or Tamil alphabet, handwoven cotton sarongs, floating candles and colourful doorstops.

For such items, head for branches of Laksala or the well stocked Lanka Hand (135 Bauddhaloke Mawatha, Colombo 3. The various branches of the Odel spin-off chain LUV SL (www.odel.lk/luvsl; outlets in the Dutch Hospital in Colombo Fort and in Kandy on Dalada Vidiya next to the Queen's Hotel) also sell a fun range of traditional handicrafts given a slightly funky modern makeover.

Tea and spices

Ceylon tea is Sri Lanka's most famous export. To sample the best, look for loose-leaf Orange Pekoe if you like tea without milk, or Broken Orange Pekoe for a stronger cup drunk with milk and sugar. Plantation-fresh leaf tea (avoid tea bags for a quality cup) is available at many roadside tea centres. There's a good selection of local teas available in most branches of the island-wide Cargills supermarket chain or (at higher prices) from the various Mlesna tea shops.

Aromatic spices constitute the soul of Sri Lankan cuisine. A specialist is the Spice Shop at Majestic City, Bambalapitiya (see route 2), or try a good supermarket like Keells or Cargills.

SHOPPING TIPS

Shops usually open 10am–6pm in Colombo, while in other towns, shops and supermarkets open 8am–8pm.

Note that gem merchants and other places selling exclusively to tourists (like spice gardens, craft shops, batik centres) build in a commission to the price they quote, so if you shop without a local guide, ask for a discount equal to the built-in commission.

Modern art in Colombo

ENTERTAINMENT

Entertainment in Sri Lanka is lively and totally unexpected: festivals and street parades, open-air art exhibitions, Sunday brunch jazz sessions, classical and pop concerts and local comedy shows add up to a vibrant cultural scene.

Although there's not much in the way of after-dark entertainment in Sri Lanka, the country has a packed festival calendar – with spectacular processions, caparisoned elephants, and drummers and dancers aplenty – and a rich dance tradition, ranging from the flamboyant classical traditions of Kandy to the populist dance-dramas and exorcism ceremonies of the south.

DANCE AND MUSIC

The classical performing arts of Sri Lanka are generally divided into two groups: up-country, or Kandyan, encompassing the aristocratic classical dance traditions of the former Kandyan kingdom, with their lavishly costumed dancers and highly stylised choreography; and low-country, covering the much more populist traditions of the south. These feature masked *kolam* dance-dramas (usually a satirical portrayal of village life) and exorcism ceremonies, which still show strong pre-Buddhist roots and continue to be a vital part of Sri Lankan culture.

Modern Sri Lankan popular songs invariably have lyrics lamenting lost or unrequited love. Much brighter and more fun is the *baila* style inherited from the Portuguese. As well as electronic bands (and there is a flourishing heavy-metal scene), oriental groups with a harmonium and hand drums sometimes play in hotels.

Major tourist hotels try to provide entertainment for their guests every night. In the Colombo five-star properties this means an electronic band playing in the lounge and a pianist in the fine-dining restaurant. Beach and hill-country hotels also have lounge-bar bands and occasionally put on shows with traditional magicians, jugglers and fire dancers.

ART

Regularly changing exhibitions of work by local artists are staged at the Gallery Café, Barefoot Café (see route 2) and the Saskia Fernando Gallery (41 Horton Place, Colombo 7; www.saskiafernandogallery.com). An art show called Kala Pola is held on the sidewalks of Nelum Pokuna Mawatha, Colombo 7, every January: around 300 artists from across the country exhibit their work for one day only.

Fire dancing is a typical hotel entertainment

NIGHTLIFE

If you want raucous after-dark night-life, Sri Lanka isn't the place to come. Only in Colombo will you find any kind of nightlife, and even this is modest. Popular nightspots include the long-running Rhythm and Blues live music bar (Daisy Villa Avenue, R.A. de Mel Mawatha, Colombo 4) and Clancy's Irish Pub (29 Maitland Crescent, Colombo 7). Clubs come and go on an annual basis: Kama (32b Sir Mohamed Macan Mawatha, Colombo 3; www.kamacolombo.com) is currently one of the main venues.

The alternative is the city's four casinos, which are open 24 hours a day, except on *Poya* days. All offer roulette, blackjack and baccarat. Drinks and snacks are available free to players, and they also offer buffet dinners and live music. Membership is in name only; anyone can sign in and play. Try Bally's Club (14 Dharmapala Mawatha, Colombo 3; www.ballyscolombo.com); Bellagio (430 R.A. de Mel Mawatha, Colombo 3; www.bellagiocolombo.com); MGM (772 Galle Road, Colombo 4; www.mgmcolombo.com); and Star Dust Club (5th Lane, Galle Road, Colombo 3; www.stardustcasino.lk).

Outside the capital, the island's only after-hours activity is at the tourist resorts of Negombo, Hikkaduwa and Unawatuna. The last two can get particularly lively during the season, with regular beach parties, discos and full-moon events.

FESTIVALS

Performer on Negombo Beach

Peraheras (parades of elephants and dancers) are held in many places, the most popular being the Navam Perahera in Colombo (February) and the Esala Perahera in Kandy (July/August). The Sinhalese and Tamil New Year Festival is in mid-April, when shops close and people visit their home villages, many to take part in contests like greasy pole pillow fights and bicycle races.

Not all the island's festivals are religious. Occasional kite-flying festivals are held on Galle Face Green in Colombo, and an annual surfing festival takes place in Arugam Bay, on the east coast. Hikkaduwa is home to an annual beach festival and Galle Fort hosts a literary festival in January.

Cricket is massively popular

ACTIVITIES

From hurtling down a river on a raft to being pampered in a herbal spa, and from galloping across the sand on horseback to indulging in wellness therapy, Sri Lanka has activities for the energetic as well as many pleasant ways of relaxing.

CRICKET

Cricket is a national obsession in Sri Lanka, and the national team's exploits are followed religiously. The cricket season begins in September and ends with the finals in April. Visitors can enjoy the benefits of temporary membership at the Colombo Cricket Club (31 Maitland Crescent, Colombo 7; tel: 011-268 1601-4). On a local level, boys playing cricket on village greens and on the beach are often delighted if you join in – though don't expect an easy time!

DIVING AND WATERSPORTS

Underwater Safaris Ltd (25 Barnes Place, Colombo 7; tel: 011-269 4012) offers wreck- and reef-diving expeditions at Hikkaduwa on the south coast, and there are also a number of PADI-licensed dive centres in Hikkaduwa, Bentota, Unawatuna and elsewhere around the coast. Bentota is the island's main watersports centre, with various places offering windsurfing, jet-skiing, tubing water-skiing and more. The west coast, including Negombo, is good is good for kitesurfing and wakeboarding.

Swimming and snorkelling
There are many places around the coast which are safe for swimming, although equally there are many other places with dangerous currents and other marine hazards – always check locally. Snorkelling is possible at various places including Hikkaduwa, Unawatuna and Pigeon Island, near Trincomalee in the east.

Surfing
The island's main surfing destination is Arugam Bay, with waves best from May to October and a variety of breaks suitable for novices and experts. Hikkaduwa on the west coast is best from November to April and has centres with equipment and instruction. Midigama on the south coast also has good waves.

Whale-watching
One of Sri Lanka's major new attractions is whale-watching, with trips run out of Mirissa on the south coast. Reputable operators include The Whale and Dolphin Company (www.whale-and-dolphin.com), Mirissa Watersports (www.mirissa watersports.lk) and Jetwing Eco (www.jet wingeco.com).

Diving in the Indian Ocean   *An Ayurvedic soak*

White-water rafting

This is popular at Kitulgala, on the southern edge of the hill country, where the choppy Kelani Ganga river provides boulder-strewn stretches of rapids. Check www.actionlanka.com for details of this and other adventure sports.

GOLF

Sri Lanka boasts several beautiful championship-standard golf courses, at Nuwara Eliya (tel: 052-222 2835), at the Royal Colombo Golf Club (tel: 011-269 5431; www.rcgcsl.com) and the Victoria Golf Club, Rajawella, Kandy (tel: 081-237 6376; www.golfsrilanka.com). All welcome temporary members – and green fees are a bargain by the standards of most other countries.

HORSE-RIDING

There is a school attached to Heritance Ahungalla (tel: 091-555 5000; www.heritancehotels.com) for riding along the west-coast beach. Horse-riding holidays are available through the Premadasa Horseriding School (11/12 Melder Place, Nugegoda; tel: 011-282 0588; www.premadasa.lk/riding.htm).

SPAS

Most major hotels boast a spa facility, with treatments ranging from the basic to the exotic. Many spas also offer traditional Sri Lankan Ayurveda treatment.

WALKING

The island's hill country (see routes 7 and 8) is a walker's paradise, with stunning scenery and a pleasant temperate climate. Many of the islands major tour operators can organise walking trips. Alternatively contact a local guide such as Sumane Bandara Illangantilake or Ravi Desappriya (tel: 071 499 7666/ 075 799 7667; www.srilankatrekking. com), both in Kandy.

Ayurveda

The traditional system of holistic health care known as Ayurveda (from the Sanskrit, meaning 'the science of life') has been practised in India and Sri Lanka for centuries. According to the Ayurvedic system, all bodies are made up of varying combinations of the five basic elements (ether, fire, air, earth and water) and governed by three *doshas* (*pitta*, *vata* and *kapha*). Rather than treating illnesses and symptoms in isolation, Ayurveda aims to treat the whole patient, to encourage a more balanced lifestyle. Several resorts on the west coast provide Ayurveda therapy to alleviate medical problems, while others practise 'soft' Ayurveda to inspire well-being. Ayurveda practitioners have to be licensed by the government, and the treatment is a soothing adventure in natural wellness therapy.

Toiling in the tea plantations

HISTORY: KEY DATES

Sri Lanka's history has frequently been a violent one – though thankfully its most recent conflict, the civil war between the Liberation Tigers of Tamil Eelam (LTTE) and the Sri Lanka military, finally ended in 2009.

EARLY HISTORY

543 BC	Death of the Buddha in India and the arrival of Prince Vijaya from India with 700 followers to become the island's first king.
380 BC	The island's first capital is established at Anuradhapura.
c.250–210 BC	Reign of Devanampiya Tissa. Indian Emperor Asoka converts the king and population to Buddhism.
205 BC	The Indian warrior Elara captures Anuradhapura.
161–137 BC	Elara is defeated by King Dutugemunu, and for the first time Sri Lanka is unified under a single Sinhalese monarch.
AD 993	The Cholas of South India capture Anuradhapura and the capital is moved to Polonnaruwa.

COLONIAL PERIOD

1505	The Portuguese arrive and extract concessions from the king of Kotte.
1656	The Dutch oust the Portuguese and introduce Dutch law.
1796	The Dutch surrender their possessions on the island to the British, who have become interested in Trincomalee's harbour.
1815	The last native king is captured at Kandy after the British conspire with his prime minister, ending 24 centuries of monarchy. For the first time, the whole island falls under foreign rule, becoming part of the British Empire.
1824	A revised form of government under Sir Edward Barnes and the building of roads open up the island to British settlers.
1867	Introduction of tea as a commercial crop for export coincides with the first railway line, from Colombo to Kandy to serve hill-country plantations.
1931	Universal franchise is granted.

A tsunami memorial at Kalutara

INDEPENDENCE

1948	Ceylon is granted independence.
1959	Prime Minister S.W.R.D. Bandaranaike assassinated by a Buddhist monk.
1960	His widow, Sirimavo Bandaranaike, becomes world's first woman prime minister.
1971	Armed rebellion by Maoist JVP in south leaves thousands dead.
1972	The country's colonial name, Ceylon, is changed to Sri Lanka.
1978	A new constitution introduces the office of executive president and brings in proportional representation. J.R. Jayewardene becomes the first president.

ETHNIC STRIFE

1983	'Black July' sees the LTTE attack on the army in the north sparking ethnic clashes. Thousands of Tamil civilians in the south are murdered by Sinhalese mobs, leading to the outbreak of civil war.
1987–8	A second JVP insurrection. Thousands more die in the south.
1989	Ranasinghe Premadasa is elected president.
1993	Premadasa is assassinated by the LTTE.
1994	Chandrika Bandaranaike Kumaratunga is elected president while her mother, Sirimavo Bandaranaike, is prime minister.
1996	Sri Lanka's fledgling cricket team wins the World Cup.
1999	Chandrika Bandaranaike Kumaratunga is re-elected.
2004	South Asian tsunami kills more than 30,000 and leaves 100,000 homeless.
2006	Mahinda Rajapakse becomes president.
2007	The Sri Lankan army succeeds in driving the LTTE out of the east.
2009	The Sri Lankan army, led by General Sarath Fonseka, defeats the LTTE. Tiger leader Prabakaran is killed and all rebel-held territory reclaimed.
2010	Mahinda Rajapakse wins an early presidential election (his main opponent, Sarath Fonseka, is arrested on conspiracy charges).
2015	Maithripala Sirisena ends Rajapakse's presidency in what is regarded as the most significant election for decades.
2016	May landslides kill more than 100 people in central Sri Lanka, displacing over 1,000.

BEST ROUTES

Colombo's skyline in the evening

COLOMBO FORT AND PETTAH

A walk through the heart of old Colombo, starting in Fort district with its grandiose old colonial buildings and then continuing on to the bustling Pettah shopping district.

DISTANCE: 4km (2.5 miles)
TIME: Half a day
START: Presidential Secretariat
END: World Trade Centre
POINTS TO NOTE: This route starts and ends in the High Security Zone – avoid taking photographs of soldiers, police checkpoints or anything else that might be considered sensitive from a security point of view.

Colombo, Sri Lanka's colonial heart, is a fascinating reflection of the island's contrasts: from the rifle-toting soldiers defending the High Security Zone in central Fort to cheery shopkeepers and street hawkers in Pettah's crowded markets; and from decaying colonial office blocks to the brash modern glass-fronted towers of the World Trade Centre and surrounding high-rises.

FORT

Fort district was formerly the administrative and financial heart of the city, occu-pied for 450 years by the Portuguese, Dutch and British in turn – some old cannons remain by the Presidential Secretariat, but there is no trace of the old fort ramparts. Repeated LTTE attacks during the civil war – including a devastating bomb blast outside the Central Bank in 1996 – largely killed off the commercial life of the area, while the presence here of the President's House and consequent heavy police and military presence means that many streets remain closed off for security reasons.

The Presidential Secretariat
Start at the **Presidential Secretariat** ❶ building (formerly the parliament) overlooking the northern end of Galle Face Green, with its neoclassical columns, steep steps and statues of independent Sri Lanka's first four prime ministers standing in front.

From the roundabout in front of the Secretariat, the seafront promenade runs alongside the Kingsbury (formerly the Ceylon Continental) hotel leading to the city's **lighthouse**. Built in 1951, it overlooks the **Governor's Bath**, a sea-

Tuk–tuks ply Colombo's streets

water swimming pool. Beyond that is the quirky **Sambodhi Chaitiya**, a towering Buddhist stupa-on-stilts dating from 1956.

King's Prison Cell

Return to the roundabout opposite the Secretariat and walk up to the security gates blocking the road to the President's House, where you can see the city's old lighthouse clocktower a short distance ahead. This is as far as you can walk, but look beyond the railings to see a small domed **cell ❷** with a red-tiled roof, where Sri Wickrama Rajasinghe, the last king of Kandy (from 1798 to 1815), was imprisoned. Turn east and walk along the road that leads past the Bank of Ceylon headquarters.

Next to it, the glass-walled twin towers of the **World Trade Centre ❸**, Colombo's tallest and most prestigious building, loom over a colonial building opposite, the former **Dutch Hospital**, recently restored and reopened, and now home to an excellent little cluster of cafes, restaurants and shops. Behind it is the **Colombo City Hotel**, where you'll find the **Panorama Rooftop Restaurant, see ❶**.

President's House

After passing the World Trade Centre, turn north into York Street. Looking west down Chatham Street you can see the **lighthouse clocktower ❹**, originally built as a lighthouse in 1857, with clock faces added to each of its four sides in

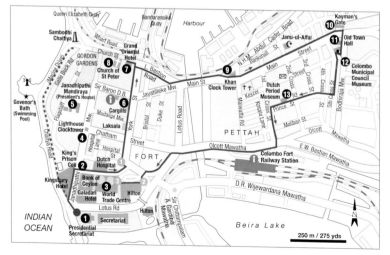

Cargills and the World Trade Centre

1914. Beyond it (but completely obscured by trees, buildings and security barriers) is the **President's House ❺**, built by the last Dutch governor in the 18th century and known variously as King's or Queen's House by the British, whose governor resided in it.

Colonial buildings

A few steps further along on the left is **Laksala** (60 York Street; www.laksala.gov.lk; daily 9am–9pm), a government-run handicraft emporium. Continuing northwards along York Street, glance up to see the puce stone walls decorated with plaster horns of plenty that herald **Cargills ❻** (40 York Street; www.cargillsceylon.com; Mon–Fri 8.15am–5.15pm), Colombo's oldest department store, established in 1844.

Another of Fort's graceful old colonial buildings, the **Grand Oriental Hotel ❼**, sits at the end of York Street right next to the port. Originally built as an army barracks in 1837, the Grand Oriental was subsequently turned into a hotel in 1875, luring in guests newly arrived by boat at the adjacent port. Next to the hotel in Church Street, behind a police barricade, is the **Church of St Peter ❽**, originally the reception and banquet hall of the Dutch governor's residence.

PETTAH

Walk eastwards in the shade of dilapidated colonial buildings along Leyden Bastion Road opposite the port's walls, and cross the small canal linking the harbour with the **Beira Lake**, passing the **Khan Clock Tower ❾**, erected in 1923.

Beyond Khan Clock Tower you enter **Pettah**, Colombo's helter-skelter bazaar area, usually thronged with dense crowds of shoppers, hawkers and porters jostling amidst the crowded streets. The name comes from the Tamil word *pettai* (old town). This was once a prime residential area but degenerated into 'the native quarter' as the British colonists moved out to build homes in the suburbs. Each of the side roads (called Cross Streets) leading south off Main Street specialises in a different type of goods – electronics, fabrics, spices and so on – with colourful shops stuffed full of every conceivable type of merchandise, ranging from cut-price mobile phones to cheap saris.

Municipal mementoes

At the far end of Main Street is **Kayman's Gate ❿**, although all that remains of the original gateway is a belfry, dating from the Dutch period. The word 'Kayman' comes from the Dutch cayman (crocodile) – crocodiles once gathered there to eat leftovers thrown out from Fort.

At Kayman's Gate, turn right to Bodhiraja Mawatha to see the **Old Town Hall ⓫**. Built in 1873, it is adorned with minaret-like towers and retains the double portico that once gave access to horse-drawn carriages. Adjoining it is the

Crowded Pettah streets

open-sided **Colombo Municipal Council Museum** ⑫ (Bodhiraja Mawatha; Mon–Sat 7.30am–6pm; free), where the exhibits include early 20th-century steamrollers and the granite slab commemorating the bequeathing of Galle Face promenade to Colombo.

Dutch Period Museum

Now dive south down 5th Cross Street then turn west into Prince Street, crowded with shops selling glass and mirrors. The old post office here was restored in 1980 as the **Dutch Period Museum** ⑬ (Sat–Thur 9am–5pm; charge), filled with colonial furniture and household items.

Leaving the museum, turn south down 1st Cross Street to emerge in the frenzy of Olcott Mawatha in front of **Fort railway station**, the country's main rail terminal. The road is named after an American Buddhist missionary Henry Steel Olcott (1832–1907), whose statue stands in front of the station.

Continue west and cross Lotus Road, returning to Fort for lunch. Options include the Hilton hotel's **Spices** restaurant, see ②, for a huge buffet spread, or one of the various eateries in the attractively restored Dutch Hospital. Alternatively, more inexpensive snacks can be had at **Barista coffee shop**, see ③, in the World Trade Centre, reached by an escalator from the northern corner of the Hilton's forecourt. Be prepared for another security check – you are back in the city's High Security Zone.

Food and drink

① PANORAMA ROOFTOP RESTAURANT

Colombo City Hotel, Level 3, 33 Canal Row; tel: 011-534 1962; daily noon–3pm, 6–11.30pm; $$

Bird's-eye views over the streets of Fort are the main draw at this rooftop restaurant, while food includes good-value buffets and à la carte dishes including curries and grilled seafood and chicken.

② SPICES

Lobby level, Colombo Hilton, 2 Sir Chittampalam A. Gardiner Mawatha; tel: 011-249 2492; daily 6am–midnight; $$$

Very popular for either a quick lunch, with an extensive range of a la carte Sri Lankan, Indian, Chinese and Western dishes, or a more leisurely dinner, featuring a variety of themed buffets.

③ BARISTA

Level 3, World Trade Centre (WTC), Echelon Square; tel: 011-233 2163; Mon–Fri 8am–6pm; $

Branch of the popular citywide chain, serving up some of the city's best coffee along with assorted snacks. Gets busy with local office workers at lunch.

A bridge over Beira Lake

MODERN COLOMBO

Hire a taxi or a tuk–tuk for this enjoyable drive around Colombo's modern suburbs, with eclectic sights that include the city's most flamboyant Buddhist temple, its grandest park and a couple of modern monuments, rounded off with a visit to the excellent National Museum and some shopping on Galle Road.

DISTANCE: 25km (15.5 miles)
TIME: Half a day
START: Galle Face Hotel
END: Cinnamon Grand Hotel
POINTS TO NOTE: Hotel taxis have printed price lists, but the fare for a three-wheeler rickshaw (tuk-tuk) usually needs to be negotiated before setting off. Western tourists will often find tuk-tuk meters mysteriously not working, obliging them to bargain for a fare. To get an idea of what to pay, ask at your hotel first, and then bargain like crazy. Walk away if you can't get the fare you want – you'll have plenty more offers. Taxis and tuk-tuks will wait while you sightsee or shop. A tip of about five percent of the fare for a hotel taxi should be sufficient. There's no need to tip a tuk-tuk driver unless they've been particularly helpful. Shops in Colombo open from 10am, so don't start this route too early if you plan to shop. Supermarkets and department stores (but not all outlets in shopping malls) are open on Sundays too.

From Fort, Colombo stretches southwards down the west coast to the commercial suburbs of Kollupitiya and Bambalapitiya, and bulges eastwards inland to Slave Island, the area in which slaves were kept in Dutch times, the broad avenues of the upmarket Cinnamon Gardens residential area, and on to the parliamentary capital of Sri Jayawardenapura-Kotte.

GALLE FACE GREEN

Start at one of Colombo's oldest and most traditional hotels, the **Galle Face** ❶ (established 1864) – worth a visit for breakfast on the patio of its **Veranda Café**, see ❶ – then drive south down Galle Road past the heavily fortified **Temple Trees** ❷ (the official residence of the prime minister) and then turn inland at the Kollupitiya junction heading down Dharmapala Mawatha.

Gangaramaya Temple
At the next junction, turn north (left) into Sir James Peiris Mawatha to visit the quaint **Seema Malakaya** ❸ (daily

At Gangaramaya Temple

7.30am–11.30pm; free), designed by the great Sri Lankan architect Geoffrey Bawa (1919–2003). Used for religious ceremonies by monks from the nearby Gangaramaya Temple, this is one of the prettiest sights in central Colombo, with three linked pavilions set amidst the serene waters of Beira Lake, connected to the shore by a narrow wooden bridge.

The **Gangaramaya Temple** itself ❹ (www.gangaramaya.com; daily 7.30am–11.30pm; charge) lies a short drive east down Sri Jinarathana Road. This is one of the island's most colourful temples, packed with an eclectic miscellany of shrines, statues and stupas, while the resident elephant can often be seen in the main courtyard. It also houses a bizarre museum (same hours and ticket as temple) of items presented by devotees, stuffed with an eclectic medley of items ranging from vintage motorcars to what is claimed to be the world's smallest Buddha state, so tiny that a magnifying glass it provided to see it through. In February, the area takes on a festive air when the Navam Perahera, one of the city's biggest festivals, fills the surrounding streets with a grand procession of colourfully caparisoned elephants.

Vihara Mahadevi Park and the Town Hall

Back on Dharmapala Mawatha, heading east, the green lawns and shady trees of **Vihara Mahadevi Park** ❺ are all that remain of what was once a vast plantation of cinnamon trees lying at the northern edge of the upmarket suburb still known as Cinnamon Gardens, dotted with stately old villas inhabited by the city's elite, and numerous embassies. The park fronts the impressive **Town Hall** ❻, resembling a miniature version of the Capitol building in Washington, DC – best admired from the balcony at **Paradise Road Café**, see ❷, part of the Paradise Road store, an Aladdin's cave of unusual souvenirs from tropical candles to faux-Victorian toys. By **De Soysa Circus** (formerly Lipton's Circus), at the end of the road, is another store, **Odel**, selling designer clothes at cheaper prices than in Europe; **Nihonbashi**, see ❸ on the ground floor is ideal for a light lunch.

COLOMBO'S SOUTHERN SUBURBS

Drive south down C.W.W. Kannangara Mawatha, past the minarets of the eye-catching **Devatagaha Mosque**, then turn eastwards (right) into Horton Place. This sweeps through a residential area of fine houses and links up with Sri Jayewardenepura Mawatha.

New Parliament

Follow Sri Jayewardenepura Mawatha for 10km (6 miles) to reach the suburb of **Sri Jayewardenepura-Kotte**, built on the location of the old town of Kotte, site of the first Portuguese landing on the island in 1505. Due to a strange

Crowds outside the BMICH

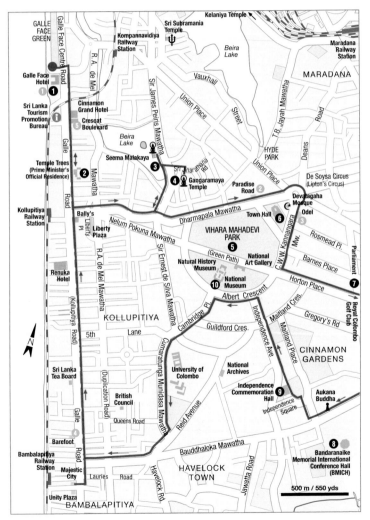

GALLE FACE GREEN

Galle Face Centre Road

R. A. de Mel

Kompannavidiya Railway Station

Sri Subramania Temple

Kelaniya Temple

Beira Lake

Vauxhall

Maradana Railway Station

MARADANA

Galle Face Hotel **1**

Sri Lanka Tourism Promotion Bureau **ℹ**

Cinnamon Grand Hotel

Crescat Boulevard **5**

Beira Lake

Sir James Peiris Mawatha

Union Place

T.B. Jayah Mawatha

Deans Road

HYDE PARK

Temple Trees (Prime Minister's Official Residence) **2**

Galle Road

Mawatha

Seema Malakaya

Sri Jinaratana Rd

Gangaramaya Temple **4**

3

Paradise Road **2**

Union Place

De Soysa Circus (Lipton's Circus)

Devatagaha Mosque **☾**

Odel **3**

Kollupitiya Railway Station

Bally's

Liberty Pl

Liberty Plaza

Nelum Pokuna Mawatha

Dharmapala Mawatha

Town Hall **6**

VIHARA MAHADEVI PARK **5**

C.W.W. Kannangara Mw.

Rosmead Pl.

Barnes Place

Renuka Hotel

R. A. de Mel Mawatha

Sir Ernest de Silva Mawatha

(Green Path)

National Art Gallery

Horton Place

Parliament

7

Royal Colombo Golf Club

Natural History Museum

National Museum **10**

Albert Crescent

Cambridge Pl.

Guildford Cres.

Maitland Cres

Gregory's Rd

KOLLUPITIYA

(Kollupitiya Road)

5th Lane

Cumaratunga Munidasa Mawatha

Independence Ave

Maitland Place

CINNAMON GARDENS

Sri Lanka Tea Board

Duplication Road

British Council

Queens Road

University of Colombo

Reid Avenue

National Archives

Independence Commemoration Hall **9**

Independence Square

Aukana Buddha

Barefoot

Bambalapitiya Railway Station

Galle Road

Majestic City

Lauries Road

Havelock Rd.

Bauddhaloka Mawatha

HAVELOCK TOWN

Jawatta Road

Bandaranaike Memorial International Conference Hall (BMICH) **8**

500 m / 550 yds

Unity Plaza

BAMBALAPITIYA

N

Gangaramaya temple ceiling

Statuary in the National Museum

whim of former President Jayawardene, in 1984 Sri Jayewardenepura-Kotte was made the island's official capital, meaning that it's this suburb of Colombo, rather than Colombo itself, which is (technically at least) the seat of national power. It's also home to the Geoffrey Bawa-designed **Parliament ❼**. Casual visitors aren't allowed inside, although you can get a good view of the building, constructed in traditional Kandyan style with tall pillars and sweeping roofs, and poised as if floating in the middle of the Diyawanna Lake.

Convention Centre

On the southern side of the road as you return to the city is Colombo's 18-hole **golf course** (Royal Colombo Golf Club, 223 Ven Pelpola Vipassi Himi Mawatha (formerly Model Farm Road); tel: 011-269 5431, www.rcgcsl.com; day visitors welcome). Drive past Kanatta Cemetery and at the roundabout turn into Bauddhaloka Mawatha. About 1km (0.6 mile) down this road on the left is the octagonal **Bandaranaike Memorial International Conference Hall ❽** (BMICH; Bauddhaloka Mawatha), a gift from the Chinese government to Sri Lanka in memory of assassinated prime minister S.W.R.D. Bandaranaike (1899–1959). Close to its entrance is a 1970s replica of the **Aukana Buddha Statue** – the original at Aukana, in the island's interior, was carved out of sheer rock sometime around AD 400.

Next, turn right into the first road (Maitland Place) after the BMICH, then left into Independence Square to see the Kandyan-style **Independence Commemoration Hall ❾**, built shortly after Sri Lanka gained independence from Britain in 1948.

NATIONAL MUSEUM

Head north up Independence Avenue, leading from the square then left along Albert Crescent to reach the impressive **Colombo National Museum ❿** (daily 9am–6pm; charge), housed in a grand colonial building of 1877. The museum's extensive collection ranges from Buddhist statues and royal regalia to kitchen utensils and antique puppets.

Continue by driving south via Cambridge Place and Cumaratunga Munidasa Mawatha, past the playing fields and campus of Colombo University, to rejoin Bauddhaloka Mawatha.

SHOPPING IN BAMBALAPITIYA

Where this road joins the Galle Road, you can detour 50m/yds southwards to Bambalapitiya to visit the **Majestic City** shopping mall, good for fashions and electronics. **Unity Plaza**, the building next to it, has the well-stocked Vijitha Yapa Bookshop (daily 9.30am–6pm) and a host of computer stores. Best of all, however, is **Barefoot** (704 Galle Road; www.barefootceylon.com; Mon–

The National Museum's imposing exterior

Sat 10am–7pm, Sun 11am–5pm), a short drive north along Galle Road. A city institution, Barefoot is famous for its colourful handloom fabrics, made into clothes, homeware, bags, stationery and cute toys, and also boasts the city's most appealing garden café, the **Barefoot Café**, see ④, which hosts regular exhibitions in the attached gallery as well as regular jazz afternoons and other special events.

The final stop on this shopping odyssey is the Crescat Boulevard, part of the Cinnamon Grand Hotel complex. As well as stylish shops, Crescat has a basement **food court**, see ⑤.

Food and drink

① VERANDA CAFÉ

Galle Face Hotel, 2 Galle Road; tel: 011-254 1010; www.gallefacehotel.com; daily 7.30–9.30am, 12.30–2.30pm, 7.30–10.30pm; $$
A memorable slice of colonial-style Ceylon, overlooking the garden patio and giant chessboard of Colombo's venerable seafront hotel, and offering a range of breakfasts, plus buffet and a la carte lunches and dinners and high-teas.

② PARADISE ROAD CAFÉ

213 Dharmapala Mawatha; tel: 011-268 6043; www.paradiseroad.lk; daily 10am–7pm; $$
Set on the tiny balcony of the Paradise Road emporium and serving good coffee and delicious cakes, along with a short menu of light meals and daily specials.

③ NIHONBASHI

Odel, ground floor, Alexandra Place; tel: 011-471 8758; www.nihonbashi.lk/odel.html; daily noon–8pm; $$
Sushi bar and small restaurant in the Odel department store, perfect for a light lunch and fine Japanese dishes during a break from shopping.

④ BAREFOOT CAFÉ

706 Galle Road; tel: 011-258 9305, www.barefootceylon.com; Mon–Sat 10am–7pm, Sun 11am–4pm; $$
Recover from the almost inevitable shopping spree at Barefoot in the soothing courtyard café at the back, where you'll find the best fruit juices in town plus a tempting selection of tasty light meals (including excellent daily specials), snacks, salads and cakes.

⑤ CRESCAT FOOD COURT

Crescat Boulevard, 89 Galle Road; tel: 011-256 4238; daily 10am–10pm; $
The lively food court in the basement of this smart shopping mall is crammed full of stalls selling everything from pizza and ice cream to Sri Lankan and Mongolian specialities. A fun place for lunch.

Inside Fort Railway Station

KELANI VALLEY RAIL JOURNEY

*This tour by quaint passenger train heads through the cluttered
suburbs of Colombo to the verdant paddy fields marking
the beginning of Sri Lanka's lush, rural interior.*

DISTANCE: 25km (15.5 miles)
TIME: 1.5 hours (or 2.5 hours including return by road)
START: Colombo Fort Railway Station
END: Homagama
POINTS TO NOTE: If possible take this route on a Wednesday, which is market day in Homagama.

Train travel arrived in what was then Ceylon with the opening of a single broad-gauge line to Kandy in 1867. With the transportation of the country's new crop, tea, from the hill country to Colombo's port, the rail prospered, resulting in a network covering the whole country. A single-track, narrow-gauge line was laid from Colombo through the Kelani Valley via Homagama to Avissawella in 1902.

In 1991, still served by a diminutive steam locomotive built in 1924, the line underwent improvements. A broad-gauge line was created, and the steam engine and its wooden carriages were scrapped. Diesel-hauled carriages now run on the Kelani Valley (KV) Line, fer-

rying commuters to and from Colombo. This is a wonderful, unusual tour for rail buffs and tourists who want to encounter ordinary Sri Lankans going about their daily routine.

FORT RAILWAY STATION

Ticket kiosk number 14 at **Fort railway station ❶** opens at 8am, 30 minutes before the departure of Train Number 9254 for Avissawella, although note that timetables are subject to change. Try to catch a morning train if possible; the latest timetables are posted at www.railway.gov.lk, although you may wish to double check in person the day before travel (or get your hotel reception to ring up and check for you on 011-243 4215). The kiosk is at the northern end of the station forecourt, on the right as you approach the station from the main road.

Fort station is the starting point for all intercity trains from Colombo. It has an old-fashioned ambience, with a wooden awning stretching its length. Hanging outside the stationmaster's office on

A railway ticket

platform 3 are antique wooden frames containing views of the railway from bygone days.

Steam locomotive

After buying your ticket, enter the station on platform 3 where, in the morning, the **Udarata Menike** is parked ready to leave for Kandy and the hill country. This is likely to be the train that the handful of tourists gathered at the station are catching.

Cross over the footbridge at the northern end of the platform to the island platform 10/11. In the yard outside a brightly painted **steam locomotive** is on display. The train leaves from one side of this platform – usually a few minutes late, once freight has been loaded into the guard's van.

MARADANA STATION

Since only locals usually use this train, the signs painted on the interior of the carriage are in Sinhala. One requests 'no smoking', but travellers ignore it. The windows and doors are left open for the breeze to blow in, and are only closed when it is raining.

As the train sets off, look through a window on the right, as you face the engine, to see another steam engine stabled in lonely splendour in a building in the railway marshalling yard. On the other side of the tracks, abandoned rolling stock peeps from vegetation while a small shunting engine putters around like a ghost from the past.

The train jerks into **Maradana station**, which has kept its original colonial ambience and railway furniture. Drivers and guards exchange gossip while more freight is loaded. As there is no lavatory on the train, the station toilet here is your last chance until the destination. The driver sounds a horn to signal departure, and the train runs along the outermost of several lines

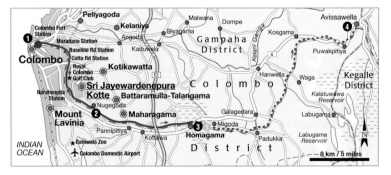

Train travellers

Going round the bend

until it veers off to the right on the single line that runs down a narrow funnel formed by two side walls overhung by trees.

ROYAL COLOMBO GOLF CLUB

You're now passing through Colombo's crowded suburbs, where the rear doors and windows of ramshackle terraced houses open onto the line.

More passengers get on at the suburban stations of **Baseline Road** and **Cotta Road**. Then the train suddenly breaks free of the shacks hemming in the line and emerges into a patch of bright, well-kept lawns and flower-filled ponds: the **Royal Colombo Golf Club**. Play stops as the train ambles across the fairways and golfers watch it with bemusement.

NUGEGODA

At the next station, **Narahenpita**, more passengers get on, only to leave the train at busy **Nugegoda ❷**, the Colombo suburb where many private hospitals are located. In this more prosperous area, vegetation lines the track instead of shacks.

The wheels begin to sing shrilly as the train speeds up and follows tight curves to enter open country. Plantain, mango, breadfruit and coconut palm trees begin to crowd in on the line, while beyond them bright-green paddy fields glisten in the distance.

HOMAGAMA

The air seems hill-country fresh as the train pulls into **Homagama ❸**, a busy village marking the entrance to Sri Lanka's rural interior. As you alight, the stationmaster hands the driver the token that means the line is clear to continue. Surrender your ticket at the gate and turn right to walk up to the main road where tuk-tuks are parked.

You can hire one of these for the ride along the **High Level Road** back to Colombo. Before you set out, stop for much-needed refreshment at the **Bonn Bonn Guesthouse**, see ❶, about 200m/yds along the High Level Road behind Homagama Police Station.

Alternatively, you could stay on the train all the way to **Avissawella ❹**, 35km (22 miles) further inland.

Food and drink

❶ BONN BONN GUESTHOUSE

Homagama; tel: 011-722 0102; restaurant daily 6am–11pm; bar daily 10am–11pm; 20 AC rooms; $
Hidden down a lane beside the Homagama Police Station, this modern guesthouse has a veranda for low-priced snacks, like devilled chicken, and drinks, with a view of its sparkling swimming pool and surrounding woodland.

MOUNT LAVINIA AND DEHIWALA ZOO

For a pleasant day's break from central Colombo, this tour takes in a morning relaxing on the beach, an alfresco lunch and an afternoon stroll through the lush National Zoological Gardens.

DISTANCE: 15km (9 miles)
TIME: A full day
START: Colombo
END: Dehiwala Zoo
POINTS TO NOTE: While the public beach alongside it is free, there is a charge for non-residents to use the beach facilities at the Mount Lavinia Hotel. Foreigners visiting the zoo are charged 20 times more than Sri Lankans for admission, but there's no exclusivity or special facilities in return for paying extra.

If your visit to Sri Lanka is too short for you to relax on the broad, and more peaceful, west-coast beaches south of Colombo, then the stretch of sand at Mount Lavinia will give you at least a quick taste of local beach life. The beach here is busier than those down the coast at Bentota and Hikkaduwa, particularly at weekends, when crowds of locals descend on the sands to play beach games, swim, and hang out at the shack-style snack bars which line the seafront, giving the whole place a slightly raffish air. It's also within easy reach of the neighbouring suburb of Dehiwala Zoo, where'll you'll find the attractive tree-shaded park that houses the city's well-run and enjoyable zoo.

The drive south from Colombo is along the busy Galle Road, with gleaming new shop frontages beside dilapidated general stores, and noisy buses and cars competing for space as they weave in and out of the traffic lanes. The steep flyover (built with British aid) at the **Dehiwala Junction** provides glimpses into second-floor apartment windows, adding to the novelty of the drive. Heavy, slow-moving traffic means that journey can take longer than you might expect: allow at least thirty minutes for the 10km (6-mile) drive from the city centre – longer if heading out during the morning or evening rush-hour.

MOUNT LAVINIA BEACH

The turn-off to **Mount Lavinia Beach** is about 1km (0.6 mile) south of the

Mount Lavinia Beach, with Colombo's skyline in the background

town's General Cemetery (which is on the seaside). Look for the Odel boutique and the eye-catching Lion Pub next door and take the side turning here down Hotel Road to reach the beach. You'll cross the main railway line south out of Colombo, so watch out for trains as there is no marked crossing point.

Mount Lavinia Hotel

At the far end of Hotel Road stands the venerable old **Mount Lavinia Hotel** ❶ (see page 90), which is also right next to the railway station – convenient if you arrive by train. One of Sri Lanka's premier heritage hotels, the Mount Lavinia sits grandly atop a small promontory jutting out to sea, separating the public beach from the more sedate hotel beach (open daily to non-residents; charge). This sprawling hotel has grown up around a 200-year-old colonial villa, originally the retreat of Governor Thomas Maitland who, legend has it, entertained his local mistress (Lavinia) here. The hotel retains much of its old colonial charm and offers a variety of splendid lunch options after a morning on the beach.

Beach life

The beach to the north of the hotel stretches in patches right up to Colombo, but the broad expanse of sand that borders the hotel's northern wing is the city's most popular. Here are several restaurants of varying standards including the **Golden Mile**, see ❶, built out of timber like a lookout platform, and **Loon Tao**, see ❷, in an open-sided thatched pavilion. The beach is equally popular for alfresco dining and impromptu parties at night.

DEHIWALA ZOO

After lunch, catch a tuktuk to **Dehiwala Zoo** ❷ (www.colombozoo.

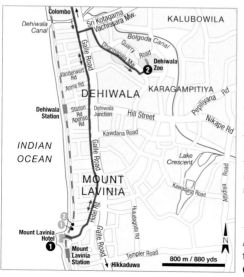

A pair of leopards at Dehiwala Zoo

gov.lk; daily 8.30am–6pm; charge) by returning northwards along the Galle Road and back over the Dehiwala flyover. After 1 km (0.6 mile), you will turn inland at Dharmapala Mawatha to reach the zoo.

Officially known as the National Zoological Gardens, Colombo's zoo comprises a spectacular spread of gardens, ponds, shaded walks, and animals from all over the world. Begun by John Hargenberg as a depot for exporting animals, the zoo was taken over by the government in 1936 and now provides a home for approximately 3,500 animals representing roughly 350 species. Arrows clearly indicate the direction to follow from the entrance to make a circular tour to see the whole zoo.

The animals

The zoo pioneered the policy of placing animals in an artificial habitat, rather than simply displaying them in cages. Here lions, bears, tigers, rhinos, giraffes and gorillas all benefit from a relatively high degree of freedom.

In the **Reptile House** you will find a rare albino cobra. Watch out for the little tortoises that ride piggyback on ferocious crocodiles. Don't miss the 500 varieties of marine life at the **Mini Medura** (aquarium), which is ideal for children. The **Nocturnal House** allows visitors to see night creatures such as owls and lemurs in their natural habitat. The zoo also has an excellent collection of primates.

During an afternoon visit you can see animals being fed from 3pm, and also hear talks about elephants, chimpanzees and sea lions. On weekends and public holidays there are elephant and pony rides (2.30–4pm). It's a good idea to escape the crowds and leave the zoo an hour or so before it is due to close, to catch a three-wheeler back to Colombo.

Food and drink

① GOLDEN MILE

43/14 Mount Beach, off College Avenue, Mount Lavinia; tel: 011-273 3997; www.seafoodsrilanka.com; daily 11am–midnight; $$$

The ritziest of the various beachfront restaurants, in an impressive two-storey wooden pavilion and serving up huge portions of fresh seafood and grilled meat dishes. Friendly service and a well-stocked bar make for a good time.

② LOON TAO

43/12 College Avenue, Mount Lavinia; tel: 011-272 2723; daily 11am–3pm, 6–11pm; $$

Rustic looking beachfront restaurant specialising in Chinese seafood including Sichuan and Cantonese-style dishes, plus assorted Thai and Malaysian offerings and plenty of other meat and veg mains. It's usually pretty sleepy by day but gets lively after dark. Free corkage.

Brightly coloured post boxes in Negombo

NEGOMBO VIA THE WETLANDS

Head north through the sprawling suburbs of Colombo to the untamed wetland wilderness of Muthurajawela, an area of unspoilt nature close to the ever-expanding capital, before continuing on to the lively beach resort of Negombo.

DISTANCE: 40km (25 miles)
TIME: A leisurely day
START: Colombo
END: Negombo
POINTS TO NOTE: This is a good route with which to begin or end a visit to Sri Lanka, offering a rare insight into the island's lagoon and mangrove-fringed coastline as well as the chance to enjoy the party atmosphere of Negombo – one of the island's liveliest beach resorts, and just a twenty-minute drive from the airport.

One of the largest towns along the west coast, Negombo rose to prominence during the colonial era thanks to its abundant supplies of wild cinnamon. The centre of the town preserves a few reminders of the Dutch period, including the remains of an old fort (converted by the British into a prison and still used as such), a ramshackle old rest house, and the Dutch canal, which arrows due north from Negombo to Puttalam, over 100km (62 miles) away.

MUTHURAJAWELA

Leave Colombo by 6am at the latest if you want to take the first boat tour of the day and see marsh bird life at its best at the **Muthurajawela Wetlands**. The first boat leaves daily at 7am, with trips continuing throughout the day until 4pm. It's a good idea to call in advance to ensure that there's a boat available.

Driving out of Colombo on the A3 (the main road to the airport), it seems incredible that an ecological haven could be found anywhere near the highway's cacophony of traffic, factory yards and container terminals. To reach the wetlands, turns of the A3 at the busy suburb of **Ja-Ela**, heading left down Bopitiya Road (signposted to the Villa Palma hotel) for 3km (2 miles) to reach the reserve.

Wetlands
Arriving at the **Muthurajawela Wetlands ❶** (Bopitiya, Pamunugama; daily 7am–4pm; charge) you'll see the compound of thatched huts housing the visitor centre where young and knowledgeable guides offer visitors a talk on

Fishing boats in Negombo port

the ecology of the reserve before loading them into open boats for the trip itself.

The saltwater wetlands and lagoons are home to abundant bird life as well as to toque macaque monkeys, water monitors and the occasional crocodile. The boat putters down the Hamilton Canal before reaching the southern end of the **Negombo Lagoon**, a breezy expanse of water running around patches of tangled mangrove swamp with egrets, herons and kingfishers perched in the branches.

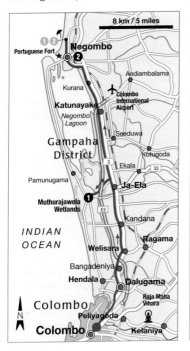

NEGOMBO

Return to the A3 and head north past the turn-off to the Colombo International Airport. Continue down a wide dual carriageway and after 5km (3 miles), turn west at the sign saying 1.85km to Beach Road in **Negombo ②**. The railway line is on one side and shops are on the other as you head into the busy town.

Bounding the south side of the old town centre, the Negombo Lagoon is the source of some of the island's most highly prized seafood, especially its large and juicy prawns. Daily fish auctions are held early in the morning (around 7am) in the busy fish markets in the town centre and at Duwa, both of which are worth

Cinnamon

One of Sri Lanka's most attractive commodities, in the eyes of the Dutch, was the plentiful cinnamon that grew wild in the island's jungles. It was in huge demand in Europe, where it was valued for its distinctive flavour and as an aid to digestion. Cinnamon found in the Negombo area was regarded as the sweetest, and hence the most highly prized. Cinnamon was so valuable that it was made a capital offence to damage plants or to trade it illegally. However, Arab traders were more familiar than Dutch naval patrols with the Negombo coast, so smuggling cinnamon was as lucrative for them as it was when sold legally by the Dutch.

Negombo Beach is very popular with local families

a visit at any time of the morning for the sight of crowds of locals haggling animatedly over huge piles of tuna, seer, mullet, crabs and other forms of marine bounty.

St Mary's Church

In the middle of town stands the stately pink landmark of **St Mary's Church**, one of the many large Roman Catholic churches that dot Negombo and the coast north from Colombo. Portuguese missionaries were particularly active in the area, converting many of the local Karava fishermen. Their devotion to Roman Catholicism can still be seen, not only in the churches, but also in the dozens of beautiful little wayside shrines along the main roads around town.

A detour towards the sea runs past the harbour, the main fish-market and St Mary's College, before emerging into Lewis Place, dotted with innumerable guesthouses and travellers' cafes. Continue along Lewis Place to Poruthota Road, **Ettukala**, north of the town, for the main beach and hotel area.

Negombo Beach

After leaving your vehicle in Poruthota Road (or one of the side roads), it's a pleasant stroll along this main street. The beach is blocked off from the road by the hotels lining the shore, so you might have to walk through a hotel lobby to reach it. This is a working beach, the preserve of fishermen mending their nets, making reed baskets or working on their vessels ahead of the night's fishing.

This part of town is one of the liveliest on the island, particularly at night: a slightly edgy place with a distinct party atmosphere thanks to its above-average number of bars and the crowds of sun-crazed holiday-makers passing through the place and resident expats – a far cry from the sleepier resorts further south. After dark, the strip of bars and restaurants on both sides of Poruthota Road fill up with crowds of western tourists. This road also has one of the island's best selections of places to eat including **Bijou**, see ❶ and **Lords**, see ❷.

Food and drink

❶ BIJOU

44 Porutota Road; tel: 031 531 9577; daily 9am–11pm (although sometimes closed in low season); $$$
Classy and cosy little Swiss-owned establishment with a skillfully prepared selection of Swiss–Italian dishes plus excellent seafood.

❷ LORDS

80B Poruthota Road; tel: 077-723 4721; www.lordsrestaurant.net; daily 11am–10pm; $$$
Attractive modern café-cum-restaurant serving up tasty and beautifully presented cuisine from around the world, although Asian flavours predominate – anything from Thai curries and chicken tikka masala through to mushroom curry.

Inside the Temple of the Tooth

ROAD TO KANDY

Journey through a cashew-nut market and a cane-weaving village, drop in at the world's only elephant orphanage and then drive up to the former royal capital of Kandy to visit the revered Temple of the Tooth.

DISTANCE: 116km (72 miles)
TIME: Two days
START: Colombo
END: Kandy
POINTS TO NOTE: Although the distance may seem short, this route is better spread over two days, as there is so much to see and do. This tour can precede route 7 to Nuwara Eliya and the hill country, or routes 9 and 10, taking in the ancient capitals of Anuradhapura and Polonnaruwa, from where you could continue to Trincomalee and the east-coast beaches.

The road to Kandy is a fascinating one, thanks to the insight it provides into the culture, religion and history of Sri Lanka. On this two-day tour you can explore a pair of botanical gardens, feed baby elephants, enjoy an energetic performance of traditional Kandyan dancing and drumming, and visit the island's most venerated Buddhist temple, home to the revered Tooth Relic.

Until the British conquest, Kandy was the citadel of power for Sri Lankan kings. The original road there was built in 1820. Now, as the A1, it is one of Sri Lanka's busiest modern highways – although heavy traffic and the sights along the way mean the drive from Colombo to Kandy can take over four hours.

HENERATHGODA BOTANICAL GARDENS

Check out of your Colombo hotel after breakfast and settle down for a drive of amazing contrasts by taking the Kandy Road at the Kelani Bridge. Some 25km (15.5 miles) from Colombo, near **Yakkala**, stalls selling the sweetest pineapples in the country line the roadside. Buy them whole, or in pieces sprinkled with chilli powder as a spicy snack.

Turn off the Kandy Road at the 27km (17-mile) marker at **Miriswatta** to make a detour for 4km (2.5 miles) down the B288 road signposted to **Gampaha**. This leads through paddy fields to the **Henerathgoda Botanical Gardens** (daily 8am–6pm; charge) at Asgiriya. Established in 1876, this pretty park contains

Pinnawela Elephant Orphanage

400 species of plants in 14.4 hectares (36 acres). You'll probably have the gardens to yourself as they are little visited by tourists.

WARAKAPOLA

Return to the Kandy Road. After the village of Pasyala is the hamlet of **Cadjugama ❶**, where women offer cashew nuts *(cadju)* to passing motorists from roadside stalls. Stop to taste the nuts, either plain, salted or with chilli, at Dimuthukaju, 51 Kandy Road, Bataleeya, Pasyala (daily 6.30am–10.30pm).

Next, the road runs a gauntlet of village houses and stalls at **Warakapola ❷**, where craftsmen skilfully weave cane into chairs, baskets and souvenirs. At **Ambepussa**, 60km (37 miles) from Colombo, is the country's oldest existing hostelry, **Ambepussa**, see ❶, opened in 1828 when the road was being built. There the A6 branches off the A1, heading northwards via **Kurunegala** to Dambulla and Trincomalee.

PINNAWELA ELEPHANT ORPHANAGE

Continue on the A1, where heavier traffic 79km (49 miles) from Colombo indicates bustling **Kegalle**. Leave the main road, heading northwards to reach the state-run **Pinnawela Elephant Orphanage ❸** (daily 8.30am–6pm; charge). There are around a hundred elephants in the orphanage, from calves of only a few weeks to magnificent, fully mature animals. Sadly, the reputation of the orphanage has nosedived in recent years thanks to repeated and serious allegations of animal cruelty, while some visitors also find the money-grubbing antics of the orphanage's staff and the circus-like atmosphere depressing.

If you do decide to visit, try to time your trip to coincided with the daily feeding times at 9.15am, 1.15pm and 5pm, or during bathing times, 10am–noon and 2–4pm. Bathing takes place in the shallow waters of the Ma Oya river at the end of the road opposite the entrance to the orphanage. Buy your tickets at the main entrance and walk down the road to the river, taking a seat at one of several restaurants overlooking the water while watching the elephants lumbering about in the shallows below.

BIBLE ROCK

Returning to the Kandy Road, you'll see hundreds of clay pots and jars on display on both sides of the road at **Molagoda**, which is known for its production of them. Ahead, on the left-hand side of the road, the solitary, steep-sided mountain of **Utuwankanda** is where Saradiel, a legendary local bandit often described as Sri Lanka's answer to Robin Hood, lived in the 19th century, hiding with his accomplices in the mountain's forested nooks and crannys between periodic raids on passing traffic travelling along the highway below.

Deep in prayer

At **Mawanella** ④, look up to see fruit bats hanging from trees along the banks of the Maha Oya (river). As the road climbs, the scenery becomes breathtaking, with terraced paddy fields, lush green vegetation and sheer drops down the cliff side. **Bible Rock** (Batgala), so named because it resembles an open Bible, comes into view on the right. Beside the road, stalls sell avocado pears and pungent-smelling durians.

KADUGANNAWA AND THE HIGHWAY MUSEUM

Climbing up to the top of the pass at **Kadugannawa** ⑤ you'll notice a slender obelisk (1832) on the south side of the road whose plaque records the achievements of a certain Captain W.F. Dawson (died 1829), 'whose science and skill planned and executed this road and other works of public utility'. A further tribute to road-making skills is the unusual **Highway Museum** ⑥ (Sat–Thur 8am–5pm, free), an open-air display of steamrollers

and antique road-making equipment laid out along the side of the highway.

Tea Fortress

The formidable granite building on the southern side of the Kandy Road at **Peradeniya** ⑦, 107km (67 miles) from Colombo) is the imposing **Tea Fortress**, see ②, where you can try and buy various top-grade Ceylon teas.

KANDY

Laid out around a picture-perfect lake amidst a ring of towering green hills, the historic city of **Kandy** ⑧ was the main seat of royal power in the island for several centuries, and home to the last independent king of Ceylon until his overthrow by the British in 1815.

Temple of the Tooth

For a magnificent overview of the city, drive or walk up **Rajapihilla Mawatha**, a road running above the south side of the lake, to the viewpoint at the top,

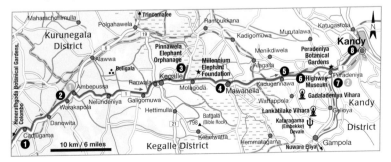

Elephants at Pinnawela
The Temple's moat

from where you can look down over the whole of Kandy, laid out with map-like precision below. It is worth carrying on to have a drink in the kitsch and eccentric **Helga's Folly** (see page 92) even if you aren't staying there. From the hill, you will see the **Temple of the Tooth Ⓐ** (Sri Dalada Maligawa; daily 5.30am–8pm; charge) rising beyond the lake. It is instantly recognisable thanks to the distinctive golden roof which can be seem gleaming above the central shrine.

The temple is home to what is said to be a tooth of the Buddha himself, brought to Sri Lanka in the 4th century from India. The tooth itself is kept carefully locked up in a casket within the temple and shown only to the most important of visitors, although you at least can catch a glimpse of the casket during the thrice-daily temple ceremonies *(pujas)* held at 5.30am, 9.30am and 6.30pm. The extensive temple complex is a superb showcase of traditional Kandyan arts and architecture – it is lavishly decorated throughout. Also within the temple grounds you'll find a small museum housing the stuffed remains of the magnificent tusker, Raja, who for many years served as the lead elephant in the magnificent **Esala Perahera** procession, held in honour of the Tooth Relic over 10 days in July or August.

There are security checks at each of the three entrances to the fenced park in front of the temple. A notice requests visitors to refrain from wearing 'headdresses, miniskirts, short trousers, sleeveless jackets and to help maintain the sanctity of the area'. Footwear must be left at a stall in front of the temple.

Kandyan Arts & Crafts Association

If you're staying the night in Kandy, it's well worth taking in one of the trio of dancing shows performed every evening around town. Arguably the best of the three is held at the **Kandyan Arts & Crafts Association Ⓑ** on Sangaraja Mawatha (near the Temple of the Tooth), where an hour-long performance of tra-

Peradeniya Gardens

About 6.5km (4 miles) southwest of Kandy, the Peradeniya Botanical Gardens (daily 7.30am–5.45pm; charge) are the island's largest and finest. Enclosed in a loop of the Mahaweli Ganga (river), the lush 60-hectare (147-acre) park, originally part of the royal residence of King Kirti Sri Rajasinha (1747–80), became a botanical garden in 1821. The first tea seedlings were planted here in 1824, nearly 50 years before tea proved its worth as a commercially profitable crop.

The gardens offer a bewildering array of tropical trees and plants plus a charming orchid house, and merit at least a couple of hours' exploring. At 550m (1,804ft) above sea level, the gardens have an average daytime temperature of 26°C (79°F) – it is best to visit before 10am or after 4pm, when they are at their most pleasant.

Scenic Kandy Lake

ditional dancing and drumming begins nightly at 6pm, featuring lots of spectacularly costumed, superbly acrobatic Kandyan dancers accompanied by traditional drummers.

Kandy Lake

The next day, take a lakeside stroll. From the colonial **Queen's Hotel** you can walk along the balustraded waterfront promenade between the temple park fence and the lake. The building on the lake's embankment, now a police barracks, was once the Royal Bathhouse.

British Garrison Cemetery

When you reach the end of the security fence surrounding the temple, cross the road and walk up the steps opposite.

About 100m/yds up the sloping road, a small granite-block lodge marks the entrance to the **Garrison Cemetery** **C** (7/11 Angarika Dharmapala Mawatha; daily 8am–1pm, 2–5pm; donation). Here in a neatly kept setting are the graves of many of the earliest British residents in Kandy, including British diplomat Sir John D'Oyly (1774–1824), who played a crucial role in brokering the surrender of Kandy to British forces in 1815. A perusal of the gravestones reveals the challenging reality of life in the then-malarial colony, with many dying young of tropical diseases.

Shopping district

Retrace your steps back along the lake towards the centre, then walk in front

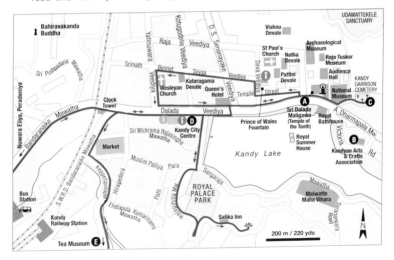

Kandyan dancing

Tuk-tuks awaiting fares

of the temple entrance and around the other side along Temple Street. Turn northwards past an open-sided Kandyan pavilion to enter Deva Veediya street, opposite an Edwardian-era block of lawyers' offices where you'll find an incongruous (and rarely spouting) **fountain** erected by coffee planters to commemorate a visit to Kandy by the Prince of Wales in 1875.

A minute's walk north along Deva Veediya brings you to the time-warped **St Paul's Church**, a relic of colonial Anglicanism found suprisingly close to Sri Lanka's holiest Buddhist temple. Alternatively, head westwards along either Srimath Bennet Soysa Veediya or Dalada Veediya to enter Kandy's main shopping district. Pride of place goes to the swanky modern **Kandy City Centre** **D**, on Dalada Veediya, although elsewhere commercial life continues along more old-fashioned lines, with hundreds of shoebox-sized shops squeezed in along the main roads and surrounding alleyways and selling everything from Ayurvedic medicines to mobile phones. For a bite to eat, stop at **Devon Restaurant**, see ③, which is always bustling.

Tea Museum

Some 5km south of Kandy, in the village of Hantana (drive in the direction of the railway station and turn southwards at the clock tower, following the signposted road to the east), you will find the **Tea Museum** **E** (daily 8.15am–4.30pm; charge). Exhibits tracing the story of

tea and the pioneers who produced it – including James Taylor (1835–92), who began the first tea plantation at Loolecondra, south of Kandy, in 1868 – are housed in an old tea factory.

Food and drink

① AMBEPUSSA REST HOUSE

Ambepussa; tel: 035-226 7299; daily 12.30–4pm, 7.30–10pm; $$

Marking the halfway point between Colombo and Kandy, this rest house is very popular with local travellers for rice and curry lunches or sandwiches in a tranquil atmosphere.

② TEA FORTRESS

445 Kandy Road, Peradeniya; tel: 081-238 7440; daily 8am–6pm; $$

Purpose-built emporium, constructed in the form of a rather forbidding looking granite fortress, selling various grades of tea as well as teatime cakes and snacks plus excellent local cuisine like grilled seer fish.

③ DEVON RESTAURANT

11 Dalada Vidiya; tel: 081 222 4537; daily 7.30am–8.30pm; $

Functional modern restaurant always busy with locals and tourists alike thanks to its cheap, tasty and unpretentious food, including birianis, lamprais, noodles, devilled dishes, and lots more, plus tasty hoppers at breakfast.

Early morning view from the Tea Factory

HILL COUNTRY

This route through tea-clad hillsides to the former colonial retreat of Nuwara Eliya offers a memorable glimpse of the hill country and provides a welcome respite from the heat of the coast, with a pleasantly temperate (and sometimes positively chilly) climate, despite lying within seven degrees of the Equator.

DISTANCE: 248km (154 miles)
TIME: Two days
START: Kandy
END: Colombo
POINTS TO NOTE: It is possible to make this trip by train from Kandy (or from Colombo) to Nanu Oya station, the closest station to Nuwara Eliya. Instead of returning to Colombo the next day, you could embark on route 8 to Haputale.

Ringed by green mountains close to the highest part of the island, Nuwara Eliya is the most popular and appealing hill resort in Sri Lanka. The town also offers a haunting reminder of British rule, dotted with old colonial-style houses and complete with a breezy boating lake, verdant parks and a picture-perfect golf course. Nuwara Eliya was established in 1828 by governor Sir Edward Barnes (1776–1838), who promoted it as a health retreat for British officials wishing to escape the oppressive heat of the lowlands. The bungalow that was originally built for Barnes was expanded in 1891 to become the mock-Tudor Grand Hotel, setting the style for other buildings in the area and turning Nuwara Eliya into a tropical version of a British county town. Even today Colombo's smart set converge here for Sinhalese New Year in April, when temperatures begin to rise in the capital.

GAMPOLA

Leaving Kandy at the beginning of the morning's drive to Nuwara Eliya, follow the A1 road past the **Peradeniya Botanical Gardens** (see page 51) and then branch off the A1 to pick up the A5, signposted to Gampola. Alternatively, follow the road due south out of Kandy until the second roundabout and take the road from there, signposted to Galaha, heading past the picturesque campus of the **Peradeniya University**, designed by leading Sri Lankan architect Geoffrey Bawa. After about 3.5km (2 miles) take the right fork, following the old road to **Gampola ❶**, 20km (12.5 miles) south of Kandy.

In spite of having been the island's capital for a brief spell during the 14th-

Tamil tea-pickers at work

century, the main interest of Gampola nowadays is the busy gateway town to the hill country's major tea-producing districts. There is a small rest house, **The Heritage**, see ❶, in the village of **Pusselawa**, some 20km (12 miles) fur-ther along the well-made A5 highway.

RAMBODA FALLS

About 10km (6 miles) past Pusselawa, the road skirts the magnificent **Ramboda**

Stunning Ramboda Falls

Falls ②, which tumble over the cliffs in two 100m (328ft) high cascades.

Some 15km (9 miles) before Nuwara Eliya, the **Labookellie Tea Factory** (www.mackwoodstea.com; daily 8.30am–6.30pm; donation) is located in pleasantly cool and breezy countryside around 1,500m (4,921ft) above sea level. The factory hosts guided tours explaining how tea is made, as well as offering visitors the chance to walk through its immaculate tea gardens, buy tea to take away or just try a cup or two, accompanied by a slice of chocolate cake, in its garden café.

NUWARA ELIYA

Another twenty minutes' drive brings you to **Nuwara Eliya** ③, the road into town swinging past the stately **St Andrew's Hotel**, which overlooks the beautifully tended links of the **Nuwara Eliya Golf Club** Ⓐ (tel: 052-222 2835; daily 8am–7pm; charge). Established in 1889, this 18-hole course is one of the best, and lushest, in South Asia, winding a serpentine course through the centre of town between houses and hotels. Visitors are welcome to play or to look around.

Drive slowly through the town to take in the sights. Before the crossroads as you approach the northern end of the main street, on the left, is a Nuwara Eliya institution, the **Lion Pub**, see ②.

Market Place

Turn into New Bazaar Street, the town's main street, where you'll find Nuwara Eliya's colourful covered **market** (daily 6am–6pm) stacked high with locally grown fruit and vegetables including strawberries, miniature potatoes, bright cauliflowers and plump leeks, all selling at much lower prices than in Colombo.

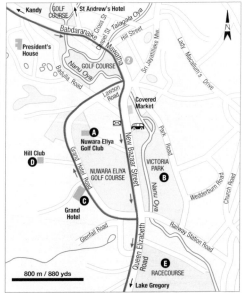

Nuwara Eliya's market

Fresh produce for sale

Stalls on the opposite side of the road sell woollen sweaters, hats and jackets to help ward off the surprising chill that usually grips Nuwara Eliya at night.

Victoria Park

The pink brick spire ahead marks the gaudy colonial-built **post office**, while opposite is **Victoria Park B**, opened in 1897 and best visited during the April season when it comes alive with blooms, as do the gardens at the nearby **Grand Hotel C** (see page 93), a magnificently old-fashioned half-timbered pile which looks like it has been airlifted straight from a golf course in Scotland. Many of the pioneers who created Nuwara Eliya are buried in the **Anglican Holy Trinity Church** behind Victoria Park.

Racecourse and lake

Follow the road as it curves past the Grand Hotel to reach the similarly incongruous **Hill Club D**, a hoary granite hotel steadfastly withstanding modern trends. Its interior, complete with stags' heads and time-worn books, is a perfect period piece, while evening meals – with waiters wearing white gloves – is Sri Lanka's most enduring colonial ritual, seemingly unchanged since the days of empire.

Returning to the main road and heading south brings you to after a further kilometre or so to the town's the **racecourse E**. The meeting held here in April and August regularly attract Colombo's fashionable set – akin to a Sri Lankan Ascot or Kentucky Derby. Slightly further

south is breezy **Lake Gregory**; boats can sometimes be hired here, and even if not, it's a nice place for a traffic-free wander. Standing on the shores of the lake and looking north, you should be able to see (unless it's too misty) **Mount Pidurutalagala**, which at 2,524m (8,281ft) is the highest mountain in Sri Lanka, towering 635m (2,081ft) above the town.

KANDAPOLA

One of Sri Lanka's most memorable places to stay – and worth a visit even if you're not overnighting here – the **Heritance Tea Factory Hotel** (see page 93) is located 14km (8.7 miles) from Nuwara Eliya amidst picture-perfect tea plantations around 2,200m (7,214ft) above sea level. The hotel was ingeniously converted from an abandoned tea factory, and from the outside that's exactly what it still looks like. To reach the hotel, take the road eastwards from the Grand Hotel junction to the plantation town of **Kandapola 4**, from where a signposted track leads northwards uphill through vegetable and tea gardens.

Here, you can explore the surrounding countryside on two-hour nature treks (daily at 6.30am, 10am and 4pm; charge) taking in the hotel's rose, organic vegetable and tea gardens. Guests learn about the art of tea picking and can pluck their own leaves – which are turned overnight into a packet of freshly made tea ready for you to take home. Beyond the hotel, walks leads past the Hether-

Heritance Tea Factory Hotel sign

sett village temple and into the nearby Kuduratte Jungle, a carefully conserved forest that is home to amazing numbers of birds, butterflies and mammals.

HAKGALA BOTANICAL GARDENS

The next day, it's well worth the 10km (6 miles) drive south of Nuwara Eliya to the prominent **Hakgala Rock**, whose sheer face rises 450m (1,500ft) above the surrounding countryside. At the foot of the rock lie the pretty **Hakgala Botanical Gardens 5** (daily 8am–5pm; charge), situated at just under 2,000m (6,562ft) above sea level and boasting a herbarium, rose garden, fernery and wild orchid collection. The gardens were originally established in 1860 as an experimental plantation of cinchona trees, which are the source of quinine, the world's leading anti-malarial drug of choice right through until the 1940s, and a life-saver in Sri Lanka's early colonial days.

HORTON PLAINS NATIONAL PARK

Beyond Hakgala, at the southern edge of the hill country and 32km (20 miles) from Nuwara Eliya, lies **Horton Plains National Park 6** (daily 6am–6pm; ticket office closes at 4pm; charge). While it is home to wildlife like sambhur (large deer), the scenery – often shrouded in mist – is the attraction. The park offers excellent hikes, the most popular being the 9km (5.5-mile) round trip from the entrance to **World's End**, a stunning viewpoint at the very edge of the hill country, where the cliffs fall away for the best part of 1,000m (3,288ft) to the plains below.

BACK TO COLOMBO

Returning to the park entrance, you could continue on the A5 to Ella (see page 64) or return to Nuwara Eliya. If

Adam's Peak

Rising south of Hatton is the dramatic mountain of Adam's Peak (2,243 metres; 7,360ft), rising in solitary splendour above the surrounding hills. The Peak has been an object of worship and pilgrimage for centuries amongst the Sinhalese, thanks to a strange impression on the bare rock at its summit that is popularly claimed to be a footprint (Sri Pada) made by the Buddha himself during one of his three legendary visits to the island. Thousands of pilgrims haul themselves up the hundreds of steps to the mountain's summit every year to pay their respects to the footprint. The arduous ascent from the village of Dalhousie on the peak's northern side is traditionally made by night during the pilgrimage season from January to April. Arriving in time for dawn, one has the best chance of seeing the spectacle known as the 'Shadow of the Peak', whereby the rising sun casts a perfectly triangular shadow of the peak's summit, which hangs miraculously suspended in mid-air for 20 minutes or so.

Verdant tea country

you are driving to Colombo, take the A7 signposted to Hatton through **Nanu Oya** (or go to Nanu Oya to catch the train). Off the A7 take the northern fork diverting to **Radella ❼**, where the Somerset Estate has a shop (daily 7.30am–5.30pm) selling packets of estate-grown tea, strawberries and home-made jam. From Hatton, you could take the memorable side-trip to Adam's Peak (see box), adding a day to your tour if you fancy ascending Sri Lanka's most famous mountain.

Back on the A7 bound for Colombo, drive through **Talawakele ❽** and glorious tea country, keeping an eye open for two waterfalls, St Clair and Devon, located on the northern valley side of the road. There are roadside viewpoints, while a commanding view of the whole valley is to be had from the battlements of the **Tea Castle**, see ❸, an extraordinary building with a restaurant and tea shop. From there it's a 50km (31-mile) drive to **Kitulgala ❾**, with its delightfully laid-back **rest house**, see ❹, offering a good option for lunch or dinner while overlooking the river made famous as the location for the film, *The Bridge on the River Kwai*. It's another 86km (53 miles) via Avissawella back to Colombo.

Food and drink

❶ THE HERITAGE – PUSSELAWA

Pusselawa; tel: 081-247 8397; www.chcrest houses.com/pusselawa; daily 12.30–3pm, 7–9pm; $
Poised over a magnificent valley view, this recently upgraded old rest house provides a reliable lunchtime option for rice and curry and other local and international dishes served in its glass-walled restaurant.

❷ LION PUB

20 Kandy Road (Old Bazaar Street/ Bandaranaike Mawatha), Nuwara Eliya; daily 11am–10pm; $
A Nuwara Eliya institution, the Lion Pub is a real slice of hill-country life, usually packed with friendly vegetable farmers in woolly caps. Beer is served and there are plenty of snacks,

including succulent fried local beef.

❸ TEA CASTLE

Talawakele; tel: 051-222 2561; daily 8am–6pm; $$
From the outside it looks like a miniature castle, but inside it is a charming restaurant for authentic rice and curry from a menu, or for a top-quality cup of tea and scrumptious cake.

❹ KITULGALA REST HOUSE

Kitulgala; tel: 036-228 7528; www.chcrest houses.com/kithulgala; daily breakfast 7–10am, lunch 12.30–4.30pm, dinner 7.30–10pm; $$
Beautiful old colonial-era dining room overlooking the Kitulgala river, convenient for a quick meal from the rice-and-curry buffet, the local and international a la carte or snack menu.

HAPUTALE, ELLA AND BANDARAWELA

Travel through some of Sri Lanka's highest and most memorable scenery, a landscape of precipitous green hills covered in endless tea bushes, where the local culture is Hindu with a quaint dash of British colonial style.

DISTANCE: 70km (43 miles)
TIME: One or two days
START: Nuwara Eliya
END: Ella Gap
POINTS TO NOTE: This journey to Haputale and Ella can also be made by rail from Nanu Oya station (near Nuwara Eliya): a memorable two-hour ride along hilltop ridges and through long tunnels, via the island's highest station, Pattipola, 1,891m (6,203ft) above sea level. From Ella you can drive south for 134km (83 miles) to reach Yala National Park (tour 12).

The route starts by heading to Haputale, dramatically perched on the very edge of the hills, before sampling some of the area's old-world colonial charms at Adisham and Bandarawela, and then finishing in the pretty village of Ella.

NUWARA ELIYA TO HAPUTALE

The drive from Nuwara Eliya starts by heading south along the A5, passing the **Hakgala Botanical Gardens** (see route 7) en route. Some 15km (9-mile) beyond the gardens, take the road turning south at the small town of **Keppetipola**. This eventually wends its way around many bends to Haputale.

If you have time, stop at **Idalgashina** ❶ and visit its railway station, located 1,615m (5,298ft) above sea level, for its stunning views of scalloped hills dropping away from both sides of the platform. The tea gardens here are organic (no artificial fertiliser is used to promote growth) and produce special long-leaf premium tea as well as Sri Lankan green tea.

Adisham

About 3km (2 miles) before Haputale the country lane brings you to **Adisham** ❷ (Sat, Sun, *Poya* days and school holidays only 9.30am–12.30pm and 1.30–4pm; charge). Now used as a monastery and novitiate by the Congregation of St Sylvester, a missionary order that came to the country in 1840,

A panoramic view of tea plantations

this Gothic, granite-block house was originally built in 1931 as the home of Sir Thomas Villiers (1869-1959). His grandfather, Lord John Russell, was twice prime minister of Britain, but Villiers was the black sheep of the family and arrived in Ceylon in 1887 with ten pounds in his pocket.

He prospered and rewarded himself for his successful business dealings by building Adisham as an expression of his nostalgia, modelling it on Leeds Castle in Kent and furnishing it with imported carpets, porcelain, furniture and glassware – the fine library remains as Villiers left it.

HAPUTALE

The attraction of **Haputale** ❸ is hard to define. Most visitors just gasp at the sight of the main street which seems to tumble off the edge of a cliff – you can walk around town in ten minutes and see where the main road skirts the long drop down to the plains below. But Haputale, in spite of its grubby streets – in strange contrast to the carefully tended tea plantations surrounding it – has an agreeable quality. Perhaps it is the town's compact size, sense of activity, and various eccentricities including a climate

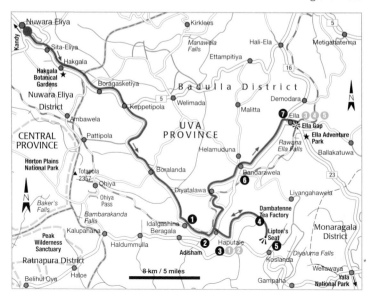

Bags of tea at Dambatenne

that changes from warm sunshine to freezing mist in seconds and the railway track running through the town centre which also serves as a market place for vendors, who have to move their wares quickly whenever a train comes along.

For lunch there is the famous local drinking den, **High Cliffe**, see 1, by the rail track, or the welcoming **Sri Lak View Holiday Inn**, see 2.

Plantation bungalows

However, the best reason for visiting Haputale is to stay in one of the time-warped plantation bungalows close to the town. Taking the road eastwards to Lipton's Seat, you pass above three of these, tucked into the hillside with views across the plains right down to

Kelburne Mountain Resort

the south coast. British planters always chose the best locations for their bungalows, so that they could keep an eye on the labourers in the tea fields below, and enjoy panoramic views to boot. To stay in one of these, waited upon by butler and cook and dining on traditional fare like mulligatawny soup, fish pie and trifle, is to taste the colonial planter's lifestyle.

The four-bedroom **Sherwood Bungalow** (reservations tel: 011-238 1644) has an old-fashioned air to it, with a garden gazebo instead of a veranda for nature-watching while having a cup of estate tea.

A little further from the town, **Kelburne Mountain Resort** (tel: 057-226 8029; www.kelburnemountainview.com) has three separate bungalows grouped around a central plateau where meals are served in a pavilion, or to the dining rooms of each bungalow.

The grandest, 3km (2 miles) from Haputale, is **Thotalagala** (reservations tel: 011-238 1644), set in a garden of ponds and flowers and with a secluded swimming pool for the hardy. It consists of three linked pavilions with a teak-panelled smoking room and log fire.

Dambatenne Tea Factory

Although it's only 13km (8 miles) from Haputale to Lipton's Seat, the drive takes time because the road is too narrow in places for vehicles to pass each other, and much of it is unsurfaced. It's

Wild flowers in Haputale   *View from Kelburne Mountain Resort*

well worth the effort, however, as the road winds slowly upwards, slaloming between immaculately tended tea gardens, revealing ever-more expansive and sweeping views with each bend – one of the most memorable short drives on the island. Alternatively, hire a taxi to the top and then walk back down again to either the tea factory or Lipton's Seat, an easy and immensely enjoyable half-day walk.

The road passes the **Dambatenne Tea Factory ❹**, which is the longest in the island at 105m (345ft). Dambatenne was one of many estates owned by Sir Thomas Lipton (1848–1931), the Scottish grocer who was hugely successful in marketing Sri Lankan tea worldwide.

Lipton's Seat

When Lipton stayed on the island he would ride his horse up to the estate's highest point, now called **Lipton's Seat ❺** (daily 7.30am–6pm; charge) to survey his tea gardens. The view from here is one of the finest on the island, looking out from the hill country escarpment, with the lowland plains far below stretching away to the coast, although thick clouds usually roll in by about 10am, so it's best to arrive early if you want to see anything.

Diyatalawa

Continue towards Ella by taking the Bandarawela road (A16) out of Haputale and then turn off westwards to **Diyatalawa**. The road winds through a forest of eucalyptus pine trees down

From leaf to cup

Following the experimental growth of tea by James Taylor at Loolecondra near Kandy (see route 6) in the 1860s, the topography of highland Sri Lanka was changed for ever. Large tracts of the hill country were cleared by British settlers attracted by the riches to be made from growing tea in a British colony. Within 20 years, the environment of the hill country was transformed from dense jungle to swathes of neatly manicured tea bushes. In time, the best area to grow flavourful tea was discovered to be around Bandarawela.

Tea begins its journey from hillside to cup when two top leaves and a bud are gently picked by a tea plucker, usually female. The freshly gathered leaves are swiftly transferred to a nearby tea factory where they are withered overnight in blasts of hot air to remove excess moisture. The withered leaves are rolled and crushed by machinery, often dating from Victorian times, to release the remaining sap and to trigger fermentation. The leaves are then fired in enormous ovens before being sifted and graded according to particle size. Orange Pekoe (OP) is the standard size for light tea without milk, while Broken Orange Pekoe Fannings (BOPF) is a small-size grade for a strong cup of tea mixed with milk and sugar.

A colonial throwback at Bandarawela

to a valley cantonment, a prison for Boers and then for German combatants in World War I and a convalescent camp for military personnel in World War II. The area has a salubrious, dry climate in contrast to the rainy chill of Haputale.

BANDARAWELA

After passing through Diyatalawa, the road climbs up to join the A16 again. The road swings into **Bandarawela** ➏ alongside the railway track. Highlight of the town is the sedate old **Bandarawela Hotel** (see page 102) built in 1893 when the railway arrived (Bandarawela was the terminus of the main line until the railway was extended to Badulla in 1924). With its tea-planter club atmosphere – a long lounge with chintzy armchairs and rooms with old-fashioned, brass-knobbed beds – it seems settled in the 1920s. Tea on the lawn served by waiters clad in tunics and sarongs is almost obligatory.

The beautiful hills around town are still the best area for what tea planters call 'flavoury tea'; pears and strawberries also reach their prime here, as the climate is drier and milder than at Nuwara Eliya.

Dowa Cave Temple
Roughly 6km (4 miles) northeast of Bandarawela, the small **Dowa Cave Temple** stands right by the roadside, but is easily missed thanks to the thick woodland surrounding it. The main attraction here is a striking figure carved in bas-relief into the rock above the temple: either the historical Buddha or the future Buddha Maitreya.

ELLA

Another 2km (1 mile) further along the A16, at the southeastern cusp of the hills by the turn southwards on to the A23, is the pretty little settlement of **Ella** ➐. A sleepy village a decade ago, it now attracts large numbers of foreign visitors, with an ever-growing plethora of guesthouses and cafes which are now threatening to overwhelm the gorgeous natural setting which brought the tourists here in the first place. The main attraction is the stunning view through a narrow cleft in the hills, known as **Ella Gap** – the garden of the **Grand Ella Motel**, see ➊, offers one of the best vantage points.

It's possible to walk up Ella Rock – a steep but exhilarating hike of about three hours return. Alternatively, the shorter and less strenuous walk up the nearby Little Adam's Peak provides almost equally memorable views.

If you wish to linger in Ella, try **Dream Café**, see ➍ or **Ravana Heights**, see ➎ for lunch.

Rawana Ella Falls
Ella is also famous as one of the Sri Lankan sites most closely associated with the Ramayana, and particularly

Early morning at Ella Gap   *Trains can offer spectacular views*

with the villainous Ravana, who is thought to have imprisoned Sita in the Rawana Ella Cave, just south of the village. Ravana also gives his name to the **Rawana Ella Falls**, a great cataract of water tumbling over a cliff right next to the road to Wellawaya some 6km (3.7 miles) south of Ella. Unfortunately, the graffiti scrawled on the rocks and the persistence of vendors trying to sell pink quartz contrasts with the beauty of the place.

Food and drink

① HIGH CLIFFE

15 Station Road, Haputale; tel: 057-226 8096; daily 9am–10pm; $

This bar, whose entrance is hidden behind a brick wall, has evolved over the years from a tiny guesthouse with bunk beds for backpackers, to a neat 11-room hotel and bar-restaurant where snacks like beef with deep-fried garlic bulbs are sensational. You can sit with locals at tables with bells to summon stewards, or have your snacks in the private lounge upstairs.

② SRI LAK VIEW HOLIDAY INN

Sherwood Rd; tel: 057 226 8125, www.srilakviewholidayinn.com; daily 7am–10pm; $

On a small side road just below the town centre, the Sri Lak's cosy little dining room offers superb views from its cosy little dining room and well-prepared local and international mains, as well as snacks, at bargain prices.

③ GRAND ELLA MOTEL

Ella; tel: 057-567 0711; www.chcrest houses.com; daily 7am–11pm; $$

This upmarket rest house offers typical rice-and-curry fare or simpler snacks and sandwiches, served in either its sedate dining room or the garden at the rear, which boasts spectacular views of Ella Gap.

④ DREAM CAFÉ

Main Street, Ella; tel 057-222 8950; $$

This is easily the best – and best-looking – of Ella's innumerable backpacker cafes, arranged around an attractive courtyard area, although there is indoor seating too. Standards of cooking are high and cover plenty of culinary bases, ranging from rice and curry through to pasta, burgers, wraps and salads, not to mention the best pizza in the hill country. Also does good breakfasts, both Western and Sri Lankan.

⑤ RAVANA HEIGHTS

Wellawaya Road, Ella; tel: 057 222 8888; $$

Good Thai food served in this friendly little guesthouse just below the village on the road out to the Rawana Ella Falls and Wellawaya. Non-guests should book for dinner by 4pm.

At Dambulla Cave Temples

DAMBULLA, SIGIRIYA AND ANURADHAPURA

A two-day excursion into the past, driving from the southernmost point of the Cultural Triangle (Kandy) to the northernmost point (Anuradhapura) with trips to the cave temple of Dambulla and the top of Sigiriya.

DISTANCE: 250km (155 miles)

TIME: Two days

START: Kandy

END: Dambulla

POINTS TO NOTE: While starting the route at Kandy makes it easier to visit the northern sights on the same day, you could also start in Colombo and take the A6 to Dambulla, then pick up the tour from there. It leads to Polonnaruwa (route 10) – or if you've seen enough ruins you could head back south through Kandy and into the hill country (route 7).

Sri Lanka's so-called Cultural Triangle – the area between Kandy and the great ruined cities of Anuradhapura and Pol-onnaruwa – served as the birthplace of Sri Lankan civilization and boasts a staggering array of ancient monuments dating back over 2,500 years, including giant stupas, richly decorated cave tem-ples and enormous tanks (man-made reservoirs), capped by the unforgettable sight of the great rock citadel of Sigiriya towering into the sky amidst the arid northern plains.

DAMBULLA

Depart from **Kandy** (see page 50) after breakfast and drive north through Katugastota to join the A9. Pass through **Matale** towards **Dambulla**, 72km (45 miles) from Kandy and 153km (93 miles) along the A6 from Colombo.

Some 3km (2 miles) before Dambulla on the A9, a large car park marks the entrance to **Dambulla Rock and Cave Temples** ❶ (daily 7am–7pm; charge), from where steps climb up 107m (350ft) to the cave temples themselves, passing an enormous gilded Buddha on the way. The temples were created by King Valagambahu, who hid here in the 1st century BC after Indian invaders had seized his capital, Anuradhapura. After regaining Anuradhapura, Valagambahu later built the temples to give thanks for the shelter the caves had afforded him. The most impressive of Sri Lanka's many cave temples, the five shrines sit side-by-side beneath a huge rocky

Buddhist statues at Dambulla

overhang, filled with a treasure-trove of Buddhist art, including innumerable statues of the Buddha and other deities, plus the finest selection of murals on the island.

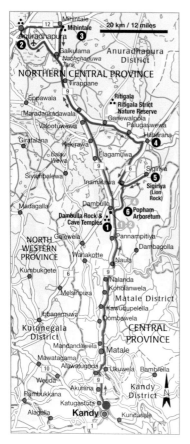

Lunch options
If you're already hungry, the **Thilanka Resort ①**, is set off the road around 2km (1.25 miles) south of the temple compound, or try the smart modern cafe at the **The Heritage – Dambulla ②**.

ANURADHAPURA

It's 86km (53 miles) from here to Anuradhapura along the A9. Sri Lanka's first capital, **Anuradhapura ②** was founded by King Pandukhabaya in 380 BC and remained far and away the biggest and most important city in the island's for nearly 1,400 years until the capital moved finally eastwards to Polonnaruwa. Anuradhapura's 113 kings (and four queens) oversaw a great flowering of the arts, producing magnificent palaces, intricate sculptures, ornate pleasure gardens and a sequence of vast stupas built to protect the most sacred relics of Buddhism. Perhaps the most impressive achievement was in irrigation, with reservoirs constructed to preserve the monsoon rains, and a system of sluices put in place to keep the rice paddies productive.

The **Sanctuary at Tissawewa**, see **③**, set in what was formerly part of the Royal Pleasure Gardens, is a good place to plan an exploration of the ruins over lunch.

Isurumuniya
You could start by heading south past the **Tissa Wewa Tank**, created by King Devanampiyatissa who, in the 3rd cen-

An ancient pool in Anuradhapura

tury BC, made it Anuradhapura's chief source of water. The **Isurumuniya**  rock temple, built in the 3rd century BC as part of a monastic complex called Issiramana, is on the right. Here you'll find the famous 4th-century limestone carving of the Isurumuniya lovers: a man and a woman who are said to represent Prince Saliya, son of King Dutugemunu, and a low-caste maiden whom he loved. The woman lifts a warning finger but the man carries on regardless.

Sacred Bo Tree

Now drive north to see the **Sri Maha Bodhi** ⓑ, the Sacred Bo Tree (daily 6am–noon, 2–9.30pm; charge), the oldest historically documented tree in the world. Because of security concerns, you will have to park in one of the designated areas about 1km (0.5 mile) north and south and walk.

The tree grew from a sapling of the original bo tree of Bodhgaya in India, under which the Buddha gained enlightenment. It was brought to Sri Lanka by Sangamitta, the daughter of Emperor Ashoka, in the 3rd century BC. Encircled by a gold-plated railing, it stands amid younger trees. Most of the island's bo trees have been nurtured from the Sri Maha Bodhi's seeds.

Buddhists consider watering the bo tree an act of devotion, so you might see pilgrims, pots of water in hand, helping to nourish the plant.

Within walking distance of the bo tree is the **Brazen Palace** ⓒ (Loha Pasada),

which once had a bronze roof, nine floors and housed 1,000 monks. Only about 1,600 stone pillars now remain of its former splendours.

Archeological Museum

You can drive to the **Archeological Museum** ⓓ (daily 8.30am–5.30pm except Tuesdays and public holidays entrance included with site ticket), with numerous fine carvings from the Anuradhapura era displayed in the rooms and garden of a time-warped old British bungalow. Exhibits include an interesting model of the Thuparama Vatadage, showing how it would have looked when still in possession of its old wooden roof.

Ruwanweliseya

Towards the north is the huge **Ruwanweliseya** ⓔ dagoba (stupa), rising over 50m above the surrounding scatter of ruins which formerly comprised the city's great Mahavihara Monastery. The dagoba is said to have been built at the behest of the great King Dutugemunu, whose battered limestone statue stands on the terrace alongside. Huge as it looks, the Ruwanweliseya is actually only the third largest of the three great dagobas which rise above the ancient city, although it is also the best preserved and continues to attract numerous local pilgrims as well as foreign tourists.

Thuparama

Continue driving to the north to the **Thuparama** ⓕ, the oldest dagoba on the

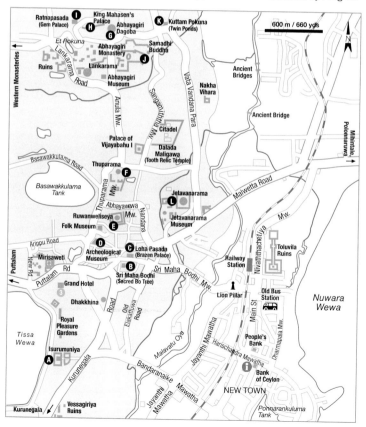

Prayer flags

Floral offerings at Anuradhapura

island, believed to contain the right collarbone of the Buddha. The dagoba was built by King Devanampiyatissa and stands just over 20m (60ft) high. Constructed entirely out of earth in the 3rd century BC, this dagoba has been embel-

lished by a succession of rulers. Its present 'bell' shape is the result of major restoration work carried out in 1862.

Next take a drive along Anula Mawatha, towards the **Abhayagiri Dagoba** **G**, which was constructed by King Val-

Elephants guard the Ruwanweliseya

agambahu (89–77 BC) and stands 74m (243ft) high. Ongoing restoration is slowly restoring the dagga to its former glory, although much work remains to be done.

King Mahasen's Palace

Close by at **King Mahasen's Palace** you'll find the finest moonstone in Anuradhapura: a wonderful semi-circular doorstep adorned with finely detailed symbolic carvings. To the west is the **Ratnapasada** , built in the 8th century, and which has two of the best-preserved guard stones of the Anuradhapura era. The *naga* (snake) king sits under a *makara* (dragon) arch, with a flowerpot and lotus stalk – two symbols Sri Lankans associate with abundance and prosperity. Return to the Abhayagiri Dagoba, turn right at the crossroads and drive straight down to the **Samadhi Buddha** , an excellent example of sculpture from the 4th century.

Kuttam Pokuna

Back at the crossroads, turn right and visit the beautiful **Kuttam Pokuna** twin ponds, once a monks' bathing pool. Drive along the outer circular road (Vata Vandana) to the **Jetavanarama** , Anuradhapura's largest dagoba. Built by King Mahasen (AD 273–303), it was originally over 122m (400ft) high, with a diameter of 110m (370ft) – in the ancient world, only the great pyramids of Egypt were larger.

HABARANA

Just 10km (6 miles) east of Anuradhapura along the A12 is **Mihintale** , revered as the birthplace of Buddhism in Sri Lanka (see box). Afterwards, turn southwards along the A9 to drive 58km (36 miles) to **Habarana** , where you will stay overnight.

SIGIRIYA

After breakfast, leave early to avoid the midday heat for the drive to **Sigiriya** (Lion Rock) . The easiest way is to turn south at the hotels' exit onto the A6 and after about 26km (16 miles), turn left at the Sigiriya sign and continue along the unmade road which gives glimpses of the 200m (650ft) golden rock sprouting from the jungle.

Museum and gardens

Sigiriya Palace (daily 7am–6pm, last entrance 5pm; charge) was built on top of the huge rock as an impregnable fortress by King Kassapa (AD 447–95), who had killed his father and feared revenge from his brother.

There are licensed freelance guides available close to the entrance to the park surrounding the Sigiriya rock, who can explain the history in detail. There is also a **museum** (daily 7am–6pm; entrance included in site ticket) dedicated to the Sigiriya story, about a 300m/yd walk northwest after passing through the park entrance enclosure

Murals   *A Buddha in the Ruwanweliseya image house*

before the Sigiriya complex.

The foot of the rock is surrounded by ornate gardens of contrasting characters. The well-preserved Water Gardens look like a tiny piece of Versailles transported to ancient Sri Lanka, with carefully tended lawns dotted with symmetrically arranged ponds, water channels and diminutive fountains, while beyond lie the wilder Boulder Gardens, comprising a small swathe of picturesque forest dotted with huge boulders and quaint rock arches.

Sigiriya frescoes

Past the Boulder Gardens, a strenuous climb up a brick stairway and spiral staircase leads you to Sigiriya's single most celebrated sight, the so-called **Sigiriya Damsels**. Commissioned by Kassapa in the 5th century, this exquisite mural, perhaps the largest ever attempted, is painted in brilliant colours onto the sheer rock face and features 21 beautiful, bare-chested women, swathed in cloud from the waist down.

No one knows whether the seductive beauties were meant to be goddesses, Kassapa's concubines or dancers. Impressive as they are today, it is thought that there were originally some 500 frescoes here.

Mirror Wall and the summit

Climb past the **Mirror Wall**, a dense spider's web of ancient graffiti left by visitors to the rock over the past 1,500 years, on the way to the **summit**. This involves scrambling through the mouth of a heavily eroded lion and then up a vertiginous metal staircase cut into the rock – not for the faint-hearted, although the view of the water gardens below and surrounding jungle is breathtaking. Amid the foundations and fragmentary remains of the palace is a large tank cut from the solid rock: water was brought to the summit using a typically ingenious hydraulic system driven by windmills.

Popham Arboretum

Drive back to the main A6 highway and head south in the direction of Dambulla

Mihintale shrines

According to legend, it was at Mihintale – literally Mahinda's Hill – that the Indian missionary Mahinda met and converted King Devanampiyatissa in 247 BC, establishing Buddhism as the island's religion. Mihintale is unforgettable: a sequence of beautiful shrines, stupas and caves strung out across wooded hills and connected by broad flights of frangipani-shaded carved steps, usually clustered with crowds of devout, white-robed pilgrims. Its various shrines are connected by 1,840 steps, all of which must be climbed to reach the summit, where the Ambasthala Dagoba, or Mango Tree Stupa, supposedly marks the place where Mahinda surprised the king as he was hunting.

Baby elephant on the approach to Sigiriya

for a further 24km (15 miles), where you will see a road to the east signposted to the Heritance Kandalama Hotel. About 3km (2 miles) along it is the **Popham Arboretum** ❻ (Thur–Tue 6am–6pm; charge), comprising 14 hectares (35 acres) of unspoilt dry tropical forest, criss-crossed by well-maintained walking trails. The arboretum was established in 1963 by British resident Sam Popham as a reaction to the widespread logging of forests. Almost 50 years on, it has sprouted more than 70 species of precious tropical trees such as ebony, rosewood and satinwood, and attracted plentiful bird life and wildlife, making it perfect for a late morning stroll. The **Café Kanchana**, see ❹, at the Heritance Kandalama Hotel is a good spot for a light lunch.

After lunch, return to the A6 to drive northwards back to your hotel to relax by the pool at the end of a fulfilling day out, or turn south for Kandy or Colombo.

Food and drink

❶ THILANKA RESORT

Godawelyaya, Moragollawa, Dambulla; tel: 066-446 8001; www.thilankaresortandspa.lk; daily 7.30–10.30am, 12.30–2.30pm, 7.30–10.30pm; $$$

The open-air pavilion dining room at this suave modern resort around 4km (2.5 miles) south of Dambulla offers a superior spot for lunch, with a mixture of upmarket Sri Lankan mains and fusion cuisine with an oriental twist.

❷ THE HERITAGE – DAMBULLA

Dambulla; tel: 066-228 4799; www.chcresthouses.com; daily 8am–10pm; $$

The smart little modern cafe at this recently upgraded former rest house provides a convenient pitstop when visiting the cave temples, with above-average light meals plus more substantial Sri Lankan and Continental-style mains.

❸ SANCTUARY AT TISSAWEWA

Old Town, Anuradhapura; tel: 025-83133/5; www.tissawewa.com; daily 11.30am–3pm, 7.30–9pm; $$

The verandas and dining room of this century-old colonial building retain a sense of rural antiquity. Great for rice and curry, light meals and snacks, although no alcohol is served due to its proximity to the sacred areas.

❹ CAFÉ KANCHANA

Heritance Kandalama Hotel, Dambulla; tel: 066-555 5000; www.heritancehotels.com; daily 6.30–9.30am, 12.30–2.30pm, 7.30–9.30pm; $$$

One of several excellent cafes and restaurants at this iconic, Geoffrey Bawa-designed hotel, offering breathtaking views of the surrounding countryside, Sigiriya rock and the Kandalama tank and above-average food including lunchtime buffets.

Sunset over Habarana lake

MINNERIYA AND POLONNARUWA

The A6 from Colombo to Trincomalee meets the A11 bound for the east coast at Habarana, making it an ideal starting point for a drive combining the elephant country of Minneriya and the ancient ruins of Polonnaruwa.

DISTANCE: 42km (26 miles)
TIME: A leisurely day
START: Habarana
END: Polonnaruwa
POINTS TO NOTE: Shoes and hats must be removed before entering the ancient temples and dagobas of Polonnaruwa, even though they are in ruins. After this route, you could spend another night in Habarana, then drive south through Kandy for routes 7 and 8. Consider taking some water with you.

From **Habarana ❶**, start early to have the best chance of spotting wildlife in Minneriya and head off along the 43km (27-mile) stretch of road from the Habarana junction towards Polonnaruwa. This is one of the loneliest roads in the area and it's not unusual to see wild animals, including deer, monkeys and iguanas, along its length. Now a quiet town, Polonnaruwa was at its zenith of power and glory in the 11th century and was the island's capital city for 200 years.

MINNERIYA NATIONAL PARK

Drive northwards to the Habarana Junction to join the A11 to Polonnaruwa and the east coast. At the 32km (20-mile) marker, a car park on the southern side of the road marks the entrance to the **Minneriya National Park ❷** (daily 6am–6pm; charge). It is best to visit the park very early in the morning or after 3pm to see the most wildlife. The fascinating **museum** (daily 6am–6pm; entrance with park ticket) is also worth seeing for its wildlife relics, including elephant and lake-crocodile skeletons.

Elephant gathering

During the dry season, as rivers and lakes dry up across the surrounding areas and waterholes turn to baked mud, more than 300 elephants converge on the retreating waters of the Minneriya Tank at the centre of the park. This massive meeting of elephants – popularly known as 'The Gathering' – is the largest of its kind in Asia, as pachyderms from across the region converge on one of the region's last reliable sources of water,

Land monitors roam the road to Polonnaruwa

travelling from as far away as Trincomalee to drink, eat, socialise and search for mates. The Gathering takes place from July to October every year (best during August and September), although wild elephants can be seen year-round in the park – and even beside the road.

POLONNARUWA

On the road to Polonnaruwa, look out for unusual yellow road signs warning of land monitors crossing the road – a startling sight as they scuttle away from approaching traffic. About 1.5km (1 mile) before **Polonnaruwa ❸**, the remains of ancient ruins and centuries-old brick walls suddenly come into view on both sides of the road.

Continue until you reach the turning south towards the **The Lake – Polonnaruwa**, see ❶, beautifully located on the banks of the enormous Parakrama Samudra man-made lake. Queen Elizabeth II herself spent a night here in 1954, and it remains a good place to stay or just visit for a light lunch of rice and curry or fresh fish straight out of the waters below.

Parakrama Samudra

Stretching out in front of the rest house, the **Parakrama Samudra** (Sea of Parakrama) **Ⓐ** is a vast reservoir of water created by the legendary Parakramabahu (1153–86), Polonnaruwa's greatest king, who famously proclaimed that not one drop of water should escape into the ocean without it being of some service to man. Today, as it was in ancient times, the reservoir is the lifeblood of the region, providing precious irrigation water for some 7,365 hectares (18,200 acres) of paddy land.

Statue of Parakramabahu/Agastaya

Drive south along the lakeside Pothgul Mawatha (Bund Road), constructed on top of the lake's embankment. After about 1.5km (1 mile), a small gate on your left opens into a park (daily; free) where you'll find one of Polonnaruwa's most famous relics: a 12th-century **statue Ⓑ** of a man holding a scroll thought to be either King Parakramabahu himself or Agastaya, an Indian religious teacher.

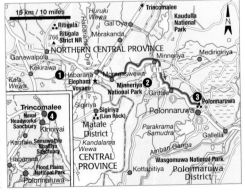

Minneriya elephants

A colourfully painted bus

Royal Palace

Return along Pothgul Mawatha to the **Polonnaruwa Museum ⓒ** (daily; 9am– 5.30pm; charge) beside the embankment to purchase a ticket to view the ruins. As you enter the main archaeological site, the impressive remains of King Parakramabahu's **Royal Palace ⓓ** (Vejayanta Pasada) are to the right. Of the original seven floors, only three remain. A staircase leads nowhere, but its former grandeur can be imagined.

In front of it is the **Council Chamber**. Some fine elephant carvings have been preserved, but even the best craftsmen make mistakes – look for the five-legged elephant near one of the entrances.

Nearby are the remains of the **Kumara Pokuna ⓔ** (Royal Baths), an exquisite stepped bath of cut stone. Underground stone conduits feed it with water from the Parakrama Samudra. Only two of the original five crocodile spouts for water are still intact.

The Quadrangle

A number of ruins are concentrated in the **Quadrangle ⓕ**, a short walk to the north. Climb the steps to the **Sathmahal Pasada ⓖ** (Seven-Storey Dagoba) on the right. Its former seven floors show a distinct influence from Burma, with which King Parakramabahu established meaningful contacts.

Next to the Sathmahal Pasada is the massive 9m (30ft) long **Gal Potha ⓗ** (Book of Stone), one of the longest and heaviest of its kind in the world. The enormous slab of stone, 1.5m (5ft) wide and over 60cm (2ft) thick, is inscribed with the great achievements of Parakramabahu's successor and nephew, Nissankamalla, who indulged in an orgy of monument-

East-coast season

It is only 85km (53 miles) from the Habarana Junction along the almost straight A6 to the east-coast harbour city of Trincomalee. The best time to visit the broad golden sands of the beaches of Uppuveli and Nilaveli, to the north of Trincomalee's huge bay, is between May and October, when the island's west-coast beaches suffer from the monsoon. After years of being unofficially off-limits because of the civil war, the east coast is opening up, with hotels being renovated for the tourist boom, while the area is also beginning to establish itself as a major whale-watching destination.

Trincomalee has one of the largest and finest deep-water anchorages in the world, and was the island's main port during the Polonnaruwa era, coveted by the Danish, Dutch, Portuguese, French and British – not to mention the Japanese, who bombed it in 1942. The centrepiece of Trinco, as it is familiarly known, is Fort Frederick, originally built by the Portuguese in 1623, and still used by the military. There is an attractive modern hotel, the Welcombe (see page 96),overlooking the harbour, as well as many guesthouses along the beaches.

The ancient Vatadage

and temple-building in a bid to outdo his uncle. A footnote reveals that the Stone Book was brought from Mihintale, over 100km (60 miles) away. The 25-ton book is believed to have been transported to its present site on wooden rollers tugged by elephants.

Nearby is the **Hatadage ❶**, where the tooth of the Buddha was once housed. Built by King Nissankamalla, its columns feature erotic carvings. Directly opposite is the beautiful **Vatadage ❶**, a circular relic house and probably the oldest building in Polonnaruwa. Built by Parakramabahu and subsequently embellished by Nissankamalla, it is perhaps the most ornate building in Sri Lanka, its outer walls carved with friezes of lions, dwarfs and lotuses, and, at each of the four entrances, moonstones and guardstones. Steps lead up to the central shrine, presided over by four Buddhas, and a central brick dagoba.

On the other side of the Hatadage are the fragmentary remains of the **Atadage ❸**, built by King Parakramabahu's predecessor, King Vijayabahu,

which once housed the Buddha's tooth. The altar opposite the Buddha image is believed to be where King Nissankamalla listened to Buddhist discourses.

The **Thuparama ❶** temple, the only building in the Quadrangle with a roof,

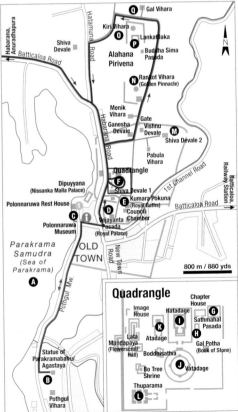

Visiting the Gal Vihara rock sculptures

contains nine statues of the Buddha. One is broken but others, made of quartz and containing mica, glisten magically in the light of a candle or torch. One statue is believed to have had gems embedded as eyes which emitted strange rays when sunlight streaked in from specially constructed angled crevices.

Shiva Devale

Leave the Quadrangle, head north and turn right at the first crossroads towards the **Shiva Devale** , a circular relic house where the *yoni* and *lingum*, symbols of fertility, are worshipped by Hindu women seeking blessings for conception. Return to your vehicle and drive north to the **Rankot Vihara** (Golden Pinnacle), a colossal red-brick dagoba standing 40m (125ft) high with a circumference of 170m (550ft). The remains of the **Alahana Pirivena** (university) and the **Royal Burial Grounds** are located nearby.

Kiri Vihara

Drive to the car park and alight to visit the well-preserved **Kiri** (Milk) **Vihara** , a dagoba named for the milk-white stucco that once covered the entire dome, and the image house, **Lankatilaka** , which has thick 17m (56ft) walls and a headless statue of the standing Buddha. Across the road is the **Gal Vihara** (Rock Temple), home to an exquisite quartet of 11th-century Buddha statues, carved out of sheer rock, including a huge reclining Buddha, 14m long but extraordinarily graceful, despite its dimensions.

It's now time for afternoon tea. Try the **Sudu Araliya Hotel**, see ❷, in the new town of Polonnaruwa 1km (0.6 mile) south, or drive back along the A11 for 8km (5 miles) to Giritale with its lovely **Deer Park Hotel**, see ❸.

Food and drink

❶ THE LAKE – POLONNARUWA

Polonnaruwa; tel: 011-5585858; www.the lakehouse.lk; daily 7am–10pm; $$
Sri Lanka's most famous rest house, set in an idyllic lakeside location and recently given a smart modern makeover – eat either in the spacious dining room or on the outdoor terrace above the water. There's an excellent rice and curry spread at lunchtime.

❷ SUDU ARALIYA HOTEL

New Town, Polonnaruwa; tel: 027-222 4849; www.hotelsuduaraliya.com; daily; $$
Bright, modern, welcoming hotel with views of its garden swimming pool and lake beyond. Set menus, buffets and afternoon tea served on request.

❸ DEER PARK HOTEL

Giratale, Polonnaruwa; tel: 027-224 6272; www.deerparksrilanka.com; daily 7.30am–10pm; $$$
Carefully crafted to blend in with its rural setting, this hotel has many corners in the garden or on wooden railed verandas in which to enjoy afternoon tea and scrumptious cakes.

Walking along the ramparts

GALLE FORT

Step back in time with a morning walk around old Galle, the most perfectly preserved colonial town in Sri Lanka, before heading off for a leisurely afternoon (or longer) on the nearby beach at Unawatuna.

DISTANCE: 3km (2 miles)
TIME: A leisurely day
START: Galle Fort
END: Unawatuna
POINTS TO NOTE: Galle Fort is 116km (72 miles) from Colombo and easily reached by rail or road before going on by road to Unawatuna beach. From Unawatuna it is a drive of 181km (112 miles) along the south coast to visit Yala National Park (route 12). There is no shade along the ramparts of Galle Fort, so wear a hat, or copy Sri Lankans and use an umbrella as a parasol.

One of Asia's most perfectly preserved period pieces, colonial Galle – usually described as Galle Fort to distinguish it from the modern city outside the old town walls – dates back to the period of Dutch rule, who seized Galle from the Portuguese in 1640 and spent the next 156 years fortifying and embellishing the town. Their work remains apparent everywhere, with streets of low-slung colonial villas protected by massive coral bastions and the gentle crash of breaking waves just beyond.

MAIN GATE

Entrance to Galle Fort is through the **Main Gate** ❶, overlooking the cricket stadium around 250m/yds from the railway and bus stations. The gate was created by the British in 1873 by tunnelling through the embankment that links the western Star Bastion with the eastern Sun Bastion, while in 1881 they added the clock tower that looms over the central Moon Bastion.

The Dutch built the walls to withstand enemy cannonballs. More than 300 years later, the fort's walls did a sterling job of keeping the 2004 tsunami at bay.

CHURCH STREET

After emerging through the gateway, follow Church Street as it curves east below the rampart wall. The long, whitewashed building on your right is the **Galle National Museum** ❷ (Tue–Sat 9am–5pm; charge), originally part of

A Galle Fort street vendor

the complex built by the Dutch in 1684 to house army officers and now home to a few rather lacklustre displays on the history of the city. Immediately past here lies the superbly renovated **Amangalla** hotel (see page 96), the successor of the famous New Oriental House, occupying an imposing building built for the Dutch governor in 1684.

Groote Kerk

On the corner of Middle Street next to Amangalla, the **Groote Kerk ❸** (Great Church) dates from 1755 and is the oldest Protestant place of worship in Sri Lanka. Evidence of the town's past is to be seen in the solid tombstones of Dutch and British residents laid out in the cemetery garden outside; the

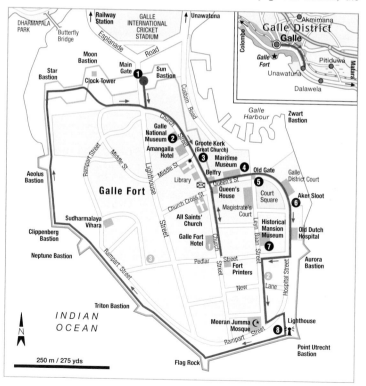

A diver on the ramparts

church's detached **belfry**, built in 1701, stands over the road at the corner of Queen's Street.

A little further along, on the other side of the street, is the British-era **All Saints' Church**. Just beyond it is the stunning **Galle Fort Hotel**, see ❶, created in 2005 out of an abandoned mansion of 1695, while further Dutch- and British-era colonial villas along the street have also been renovated and reopened as smart little boutiques – evidence of the increasing tide of gentrification which has swept through Galle over the past decade, and of the town's sizeable expat European community.

Unawatuna beach

The village of Unawatuna is spread out around a picture-perfect bay. Formerly the most popular beachside hangout in Sri Lanka and a long-established backpacker favourite, the village is now beginning to suffer from years of overdevelopment – and from the increasingly huge crowds of tourists who descend on the place – but remains a pleasant spot to while away a day or two, with an excellent selection of guesthouses and cafés, pleasantly laid-back by day, and with a distinct party atmosphere after dark, as the beachfront bars fire up into life. There's also reasonable swimming plus a bit of snorkelling and surfing (although not as good as at other places around the island, such as nearby Hikkaduwa).

QUEEN'S STREET

Retrace your steps for a few yards then turn right down Queen's Street where the **Queen's House** opposite the Groote Kerk belfry boldly displays the date ANNO 1683. Diagonally opposite is the town's modern but disappointing **Maritime Museum** ❹ (daily 9am–5pm; charge), housed in the sprawling Great Warehouse, one of Galle's biggest and most-eyeing catching colonial buildings.

Built up against the end of the Great Warehouse is the fort's **Old Gate** ❺, which has the novelty of two competing crests: a VOC Dutch crest (dated ANNO MDCLXIX) above the gate on the inside of the fort, and a British coat of arms, added at a later date, on the gate's exterior face.

AKER SLOOT

Walk back through the gate into the fort and skirt round to the eastern corner of Court Square, where the date 1759 etched into a white wall identifies the **Aker Sloot** ❻. Still a government residence, the breadfruit tree above its high walls was introduced by the Dutch – the first of its kind on the island. South of here, along Hospital Street, the long white building on the sea-facing side of the street is the old Dutch Hospital.

Historical Mansion Museum

A block inland, on Leyn Baan Street, is the quirky **Historical Mansion**

Dutch-era architecture   *Stopping for a rest*

Museum ❼ (daily 9am–6pm, closed Friday noon–2pm; free), comprising several rooms of random bric-a-brac collected by its owner over the past forty-plus years. Local artisans including lace-makers and gem-cutters can also often been seen at work on the premises. **Serendipity Arts Café**, see ❷ is a good option if you are in need of refreshment, or turn down Pedlar Street to try **Pedlar's Inn Café**, see ❸.

THE RAMPARTS

South of here, Leyn Baan Street continues to the seafront ramparts and the 18m (59ft) **lighthouse** ❽ at the Point Utrecht Bastion, built in 1940 to replace the old British lighthouse that burnt down in 1936. Although you can't climb it, you can step up to the top of the rampart wall and walk along the grass embankment – popular with local snake-charmers who often set up shop here. On the landside is the white, Baroque-looking **Meeran Jumma Mosque**.

From here, you can walk along the embankment parallel to Rampart Street with the sea on one side and the red-tiled rooftops of the tiny houses crammed into the fort on the other. Steps lead down from the ramparts to pockets of beach where families splash in the sea and couples snuggle under umbrellas.

After the **Aeolus Bastion**, the ramparts broaden and provide a breezy walk past the **Star Bastion** to the **clock tower** and back to the Main Gate.

UNAWATUNA

Grab a three-wheeler taxi and travel for 5km (3 miles) east along the south coast to **Unawatuna beach** (see box) for lunch (see page 103) and a swim.

Food and drink

❶ GALLE FORT HOTEL
28 Church Street; tel: 091-223 2870, www.galleforthotel.com; daily 12.30am–10pm; $$$$
The superb Galle Fort Hotel's memorable courtyard provides a suitably stylish home for Sri Lanka's best fusion cuisine, full of bright, strong flavours. There's also a snack menu available at lunchtime, plus homemade cakes in the afternoon, accompanied by fine coffee.

❷ SERENDIPITY ARTS CAFÉ
Leyn Baan Street; tel: 091-224 6815; daily 7.30am–9.30pm; $$
Popular and funky little café serving up all sorts of breakfasts, plus sandwiches, wraps, cakes and a short selection of international mains with a mostly Asian twist.

❸ PEDLAR'S INN CAFÉ
92 Pedlar Street; tel: 091-222 5333, www.pedlarsinn.com; daily 9am–9.30pm; $$
Small informal café with delicious snacks, juices, coffee and tea served on a verandah. Brilliant spot for a break while watching the life of Galle Fort pass by.

In Yala National Park

YALA NATIONAL PARK

The jewel in Sri Lanka's wildlife crown, magnificent Yala National Park provides a memorable showcase of the island's fauna, with troupes of elephants, gaping crocodiles and one of the planet's largest leopard populations, offering an unrivalled opportunity to see this most elusive of big cats in the wild.

DISTANCE: 67km (42 miles)
TIME: A full day
START: Hambantota
END: Yala National Park
POINTS TO NOTE: The best way to visit the park is to take an early jeep tour at around 6am to view bird life, or at around 3pm for elephants. Leopards can sometimes be seen, but sloth bears are elusive. The park is closed every year from 1 September to 16 October, when animals move elsewhere in search of water. This tour follows route 11 if you take the A2 for 128km (80 miles) east from Galle; alternatively, after route 8 drive 88km (55 miles) south from Ella on the A23/A2 to pick it up at Tissamaharama.

The most famous of Sri Lanka's 22 national parks, Yala covers a vast swathe of countryside in the southeast of the island beyond Tissamaharama, protecting a diverse range of habitats including scrub jungle, tanks, brackish lagoons and swamps. Much of the park is closed to visitors, but the area which is open has probably the richest and most varied collection of wildlife in the country, and is the best park in the country for viewing the biggest variety of mammals in a single day. Wildlife includes a substantial elephant population, elusive sloth bears, gorgeous bird life and, most famously, a significant leopard population. Although they're not easy to spot, you've reasonable odds of seeing one if you spend some time in the park with a reputable outfit.

HAMBANTOTA

Around 50 miles (80 km) east from Galle, the town of **Hambantota** ❶ was the focus for massive development during the tenure of former president and local son Mahinda Rajapakse, with projects including the construction of a massive Chinese-sponsored port and the island's second international airport. Turn off the highway that bypasses Hambantota to drive into the town, one of the biggest along

A green bee-eater in the park

the south coast. The town has Sri Lanka's largest population of Malay Muslims – its name is said to derive from *sampans*, the boats that the Malays arrived in, and *tota*, or harbour. You will notice an unusually large number of mosques here, as well as the occasional East Asian-looking face amid the Sri Lankan crowds.

Hambantota is also known as the island's major centre of salt production, which is collected from the enormous evaporating salt pans that ring the town, and for its curd. Made from buffalo milk, it is sold from many roadside stalls and makes a delicious treat – look for the strings of clay pots hanging up outside local shops. For refreshment try the **Hambantota Rest House**, see ❶.

TISSAMARAHAMA

Return to the coastal road to drive through lush, low vegetation that gives way to thorny plants and small shrubs, typical of the dry zone. After 15km (9 miles) the road passes **Bundala National Park**, famed for its aquatic bird life, particularly the enormous flocks of flamingoes which can often be seen here. Beyond here, the road gradually turns inland towards **Tissamaharama** ❷ (or 'Tissa', as it's usually called), one of the most historic towns in the south. Under the name of Mahagama it formerly served as the capital of southern Sri Lanka during the Anuradhapuran period, and still has a pair of huge stupas and a collection of ancient tanks.

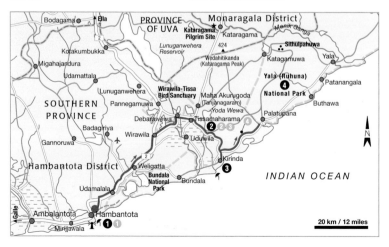

On a jeep safari

Safari jeeps

If you are not going to stay close to Yala, safaris can easily be arranged in Tissa, or you can arrange to be picked up at the Rajapakse international airport by the **Yala Safari Camping team** (www.srilankayalasafari.cm; tel: 077 3175 482).

There are many guesthouses in the town; try lakeside **The Safari**, see ② for lunch, or alternatively, head to nearby **Refresh**, see ③ restaurant.

KIRINDA

To reach Yala National Park, set off southwards towards the coast along the road to Kirinda, 10km (6 miles) away. At **Kirinda** ③ there is a lovely view of the southern coast from a temple atop a rock. This is the spot where Vihara Mahadevi, the mother of the Sinhalese hero Dutugemunu, is said to have landed after she been cast adrift at sea in a boat as a sacrifice by her father to placate angry gods who had caused the sea to rise, flooding the coast – an ancient legend which perhaps encapsulates memories of an earlier Sri Lankan tsunami.

Signs of human habitation become sparse as the road winds for another 33km (21 miles) along the coast through scrubland, salt pans and swamps where buffaloes wallow. Watch out for peacocks preening themselves and the grey silhouettes of wild elephants, looking like boulders, in the distance. Just before the entrance to the park is a signpost to the **Cinnamon Wild Yala** resort, see ④, the closest hotel to the park and the most convenient place to stay or have a meal. Safaris can be arranged with the drivers of jeeps parked at the hotel's gate.

YALA NATIONAL PARK

By hired jeep it takes about 10 minutes to drive to the **Yala National Park** ④ from the Cinnamon Wild Yala hotel. There is a small museum near the entrance showing the development of the park, as well as models and skeletons of animals found there.

In addition to the entrance fee, you have to pay a tracker assigned by the park. The trackers are experienced in the ways of the jungle and sometimes prove to be fascinating companions, spotting the best places to find wildlife, including herds of deer, buffaloes, crocodiles, sambhurs, monkeys, flying squirrels and birds that migrate from India and as far afield as Europe including painted stork, heron, ibis, green bee-eater, green pigeon and Malabar pied hornbill. These spots are usually near waterholes, where animals come to drink in the evening and early morning.

Elephants and leopards

The greatest thrill, however, is the sight of wild elephants and leopards. The elephant found in Sri Lanka belongs

A thirsty leopard stops for refreshment

to the same subspecies as that found throughout Asia. These huge creatures move majestically and are seldom bothered about visitors, except when they feel threatened. The real highlight of Yala is its remarkable population of leopards, reckoned to be the densest anywhere in the world, with 60–70 animals living in the area of the park open to visitors. Sightings of these notoriously difficult-to-spot and largely nocturnal animals are far from guaranteed, but spend a day in the park and you've got a reasonable chance, with animals sometimes seen sat atop the various rock outcrops which dot the park preening themselves in the sun, dangling from the branches of a tree overhead, or occasionally sauntering casually down one of the park's dirt tracks.

Food and drink

① HAMBANTOTA REST HOUSE

Hambantota; tel: 047-222 0299; daily noon–3pm, 7–10pm; $$

Engagingly time-warped government rest house with fine views of the harbour below and coastal sand dunes beyond. The dining room is a fine old colonial period piece offering a range of reasonably prepared and inexpensive à la carte dishes including fresh fish and the inevitable rice and curry, served in huge portions.

② THE SAFARI

Tissamaharama; tel: 011-558 58 58; www.chcresorts.com; daily 12.30–3pm, 7.30–10.30pm; $$$

Overlooking the shores of the idyllic Tissa Wewa lake, this long-established resort, recently given a major makeover and upgrade, is a decent spot for lunch, with a good selection of local and international mains, including fish fresh out of the adjacent lake.

③ REFRESH

Akurugoda, Tissamaharama; tel: 047-223 7357; daily 5am–10.30pm; $$$

This large and always-busy restaurant is an almost obligatory port of call for all tourists visiting Tissa, set in a spacious outdoor pavilion. The huge menu features all sorts of Sri Lanka and international dishes with various levels of success, although the fish and seafood is usually pretty good, and the huge rice and curry spreads are amongst the best in the country, all delivered with efficient and friendly service.

④ CINNAMON WILD YALA

Kirinda, Tissamaharama; tel: 047-223 9450; www.cinnamonwildyala.com/ cinnamonwildyala; daily 7–10.30am, 12.30–3pm, 7.30–10.30pm; $$$$

Long-running jungle resort (formerly Yala Village) where elephants often pop in. Choose from snacks in its poolside lounge bar and buffets with a wide selection of Western and Eastern dishes in the open-sided restaurant with views out over the jungle.

DIRECTORY

Hand-picked hotels and restaurants to suit all budgets and tastes, organised by area, plus an alphabetical listing of practical information, a language guide and an overview of the best books and films to give you a flavour of the country.

One of Casa Colombo's luxurious rooms

ACCOMMODATION

There is a broad range of accommodation available throughout the country, from budget guesthouses to expensive, super-chic boutique villas, by way of government-operated rest houses and luxe five-star palaces.

Independent travellers can usually find walk-in accommodation or book through a local travel agent. Sri Lanka has three major local hotel chains: Cinnamon Hotels (www.cinnamonhotels. com), Aitken Spence Hotels (www. aitkenspencehotels.com) and Jetwing Hotels (www.jetwinghotels.com). All run their properties to a high standard. However, despite the continual opening of new hotels and guesthouses, Sri Lanka still struggles to accommodate the increasingly large number of visitors flocking to the island, and in popular tourist destinations from November to March, rooms can be in very short supply indeed (although from April to October things are much quieter). If travelling during peak season it's well worth booking ahead – and if you want to stay in a particular hotel or guest-

house, try to book at least a month ahead. If you do arrive somewhere without a reservation, it generally pays to avoid the suggestions of touts and tuktuk drivers, who will either be trying to flog substandard accommodation or take you to a place where they get commission – which will then be added to your bill.

Rates are for a standard double room per night, including breakfast, but not including local taxes (usually 17 percent) and service charge (an extra 10 percent on the room rate plus tax).

Colombo

Casa Colombo
231 Galle Road, Colombo 4; tel: 011-452 0130; www.casacolombo.com; $$$$
Colombo's funkiest place to stay, occupying a patrician old colonial mansion which has been given a hip makeover with lots of quirky modern touches – watch out for the pink pool and glass sunbeds. Each of the 12 individually designed suites comes equipped with all mod-cons and latest high-tech gadgets, such as iPod docking stations.

Cinnamon Grand
77 Galle Road, Colombo 3; tel: 011-243 7437; www.cinnamonhotels.com; $$$
Colombo's grandest hotel, with plenty of five-star glitz and style, although rates

Price for a double room for one night with breakfast:
$$$$ = over $250
$$$ = $150–250
$$ = $50–150
$ = below $50

The GEM suite at Jetwing's St Andrew's

are surprisingly affordable. In-house facilities include the city's best selection of restaurants and the lovely Angsana Spa, while rooms are attractively furnished, and come with great views over downtown Colombo.

Galle Face Hotel

2 Galle Road, Colombo 3; tel: 011-254 1010; www.gallefacehotel.com; $$
Famous old colonial landmark in a peerless position on the oceanfront at the southern end of Galle Face Green. The hotel has bags of atmosphere, although rooms in the old wing are a bit musty and old-fashioned; those in the newly restored Regency Wing combine modern comforts with colonial grace. There's also a beautiful new spa, and several appealing restaurants and bars.

Lake Lodge

20 Alvis Terrace, Colombo 3; tel: 011 232 6443; www.taruhotels.com; $$$
Long-running Slave Island guesthouse which has recently been given a cool contemporary makeover by leading Sri Lankan designer Taru. Scores highly for it stylish rooms and central but peaceful location – and rates are surprisingly inexpensive.

Hotel Renuka & Renuka City Hotel

328 Galle Road, Colombo 3; tel: 011-257 3598; www.renukahotel.com; $$$
Functional and comfortable business-oriented pair of linked hotels on the Galle Road, conveniently central for the southern suburbs, although road noise can be intrusive – get a room at the back, if possible. There's also a small swimming pool, while the Palmyrah restaurant is known for its excellent Sri Lankan cuisine, including Jaffna-style specialities.

Taj Samudra

25 Galle Face Green, Colombo 3; tel: 011 244 6622; www.tajhotels.com; $$$$
One of the top hotels in Colombo, with an excellent location right on Galle Face Green, sweeping public areas and a selection of excellent restaurants (including the Navratna, perhaps the best North Indian restaurant in the country). More expensive rooms have superb views across Galle Face Green and the ocean; facilities include a health club and squash and tennis courts.

Tintagel

65 Rosmead Place, Colombo 7; tel: 011-460 2122; www.paradiseroadhotels.com; $$$$
Luxurious boutique hotel occupying the atmospheric colonial mansion which was formerly the family home of the Bandaranaike family, who have provided Sri Lanka with three prime ministers since Independence. Accommodation is in one of ten gorgeous suites, while facilities include a picture-perfect little infinity pool and a very chi-chi in-house restaurant and bar.

Jetwing Beach's terrace

Around Colombo: Mount Lavinia

Mount Lavinia

100 Hotel Road, Mount Lavinia; tel: 011-271 1711; www.mountlaviniahotel.com; $$$

One of Sri Lanka's most famous old hotels, this sprawling white landmark grew up around a 19th-century governor's love nest. Modern extensions have all but swallowed up the original mansion, but the hotel retains enough colonial touches to set it apart from the run-of-the-mill west-coast resorts. It has a superb private beach, a gorgeous Ayurveda centre and top-class food. Don't miss the Seafood Cove for fresh fish and crustaceans cooked as you like and served on the beach.

West Coast: Negombo

Icebear Hotel

103 Lewis Place; tel: 031 223 3862; www.icebearhotel.com; $$

Sociable and good-value little Swiss-owned guesthouse. It's eight rooms are attractively furnished in mock-colonial style and there's plenty of space for idle lounging in the lovely beachfront garden.

Jetwing Ayurveda Pavilions

Ethukala, Negombo; tel: 031 227 6719; www.jetwinghotels.com; $$$$

Beautifully intimate little boutique Ayurveda hotel, with a range of courses and treatments and an army of therapists on hand to purge your system and balance your *doshas* (although you can

also stay here without taking any treatments if you like). Accommodation is in beautiful self-contained bungalows with private garden, each discreetly hidden behind high ochre walls.

Jetwing Beach

Ethulkala, Negombo; tel: 031-227 3500; www.jetwinghotels.com; $$$$

Negombo's only five-star hotel, on a busy strip of beach at the northern end of the resort area, with superbly designed (but low-ceilinged) rooms, elegantly furnished with lots of dark wood, crisp white sheets and glass-walled bathrooms. There's also excellent food and a big pool.

West Coast: Bentota

Avani Bentota Resort & Spa

Bentota beach; tel: 034 494 7878, www.serendibleisure.com; $$$$

Serene resort (formerly known as the Serendib Hotel) set in a low, elegant white building on a pleasantly wide stretch of Bentota beach. The whole place has recently been given a stylish upgrade, with beautifully refurbished rooms and a fancy spa, although the atmosphere remains pleasantly laid-back compared to the busier resorts further up the coast.

Club Villa

138/15 Galle Road; tel: 034 227 5312; www.club-villa.com; $$$$

One of Sri Lanka's most attractive boutique hotels, set in a cluster of gorgeous

Sunset dining at Jetwing Beach

Geoffrey Bawa-designed colonial-style buildings behind a garden running down to the beach. The place manages to combine style and luxury with a pleasantly informal atmosphere – a perfect place to kill a few days lolling around in the sun and filling up on the hotel's excellent cooking.

Paradise Road The Villa

138/18 Galle Road; tel: 034 227 5311; www.paradiseroadhotels.com; $$$$

Alluring bolt-hole, occupying the superb Mohotti Walauwe, a fine old colonial-era mansion which was restyled by Geoffrey Bawa in the 1970s and has now been given another makeover by Paradise Road style-guru Shanth Fernando. The whole place is a model of stylish intimacy, with chic but comfortable rooms, a gorgeous pool and lovely gardens running down to the sea.

Saman Villas

Aturuwella; tel: 034 227 5435; www.samanvilla.com; $$$$

Ultra-luxurious boutique hotel superbly situated on the headland dividing Bentota and Induruwa beaches, with wonderful views in either direction and a superb infinity pool built at the edge of the bluff, which seems to hover in mid-air. Rooms, within individual chalets, lack the style of other places nearby but come equipped with every conceivable mod con. There's also a fabulous spa, exquisitely designed in quasi-Japanese style.

Shangri-Lanka Villa

23 De Alwis Road, Horanduwa; tel: 034 227 1181; www.shangrilankavilla.com; $$

Tucked away in a lovely garden with pool, this tiny 'boutique guesthouse' has just three rooms, offering a peaceful hideaway and great value in a very welcoming atmosphere.

Hotel Susanthas

Nikethana Road, Pitaramba, Bentota; tel: 034-227 5324; $$

Reliable budget option, just behind the railway station and a very short walk from the beach, with pleasant, simple rooms (some with air conditioning) around a shady central courtyard.

West Coast: Ahungalla

Heritance Ahungalla

Ahungalla; tel: 091-555 5000; www.heritancehotels.com; $$$$

Nestled amid a sea of palm trees, this luxurious Geoffrey-Bawa designed five-star is large but cleverly laid-out to preserve a sense of intimacy, with interlinked buildings backing a huge infinity pool which seems to blend magically with the sea.

West Coast: Hikkaduwa

Asian Jewel

Baddegama Road; tel: 091 493 1388, www.asian-jewel.com; $$$$

A real gem of a boutique hotel, set on the shores of panoramic Bird Lake just a few minutes inland from Hikkaduwa.

A room at St Andrew's

Rooms are decorated in colonial style and set amidst beautiful gardens, and the food is top-notch.

Cultural Triangle: Kandy

Amaya Hills

Heerassagala; tel: 081 447 4022; www.amayaresorts.com; $$$$

Large pink hotel perched way up in the hills a few kilometres outside Kandy. The setting is gorgeous and the comfortable rooms are cheerfully furnished with colourful Kandyan-style touches. There's also a swimming pool (though it can get chilly up here), and an attractive spa.

Earl's Regency

Kundasale, Kandy; tel: 081 242 2122; www.aitkenspencehotels.com/earlsregency; $$$$

This large and swanky five-star hotel about 4km (2.5 miles) outside Kandy has a beautiful scenic setting by the Mahaweli Ganga, although the whole place sometimes seems a bit out of proportion with its rural setting. Rooms are plush and the service is tip-top, while facilities include a swimming pool, tennis courts, a gym and a health and Ayurveda centre.

Helga's Folly

32 Frederick E. Silva Mawatha, Kandy; tel: 081-223 4571; www.helgasfolly.com; $$$

Marvellously maverick hotel, set in a glorious position high above Kandy. The interior is like a kind of eccentric museum, filled with huge quantities of bric-a-brac ranging from animal heads and colonial photos to Indonesian puppets and huge candles covered in clumps of solidified wax. All rooms are individually decorated with colourful murals. The dispensary bar, cluttered nooks and crannies, laidback service, absence of package tourists, and occasional appearances by Madame Helga herself, are all part of the charm.

The Kandy House

Amunugama Walauwa, Gunnepana; tel: 081 492 1394; www.thekandyhouse.com; $$$$

One of the island's most magical boutique hotels, occupying a wonderfully atmospheric old traditional manor house tucked away in peaceful countryside 5km (3 miles) from Kandy. Rooms are beautifully furnished in traditional style, and there's good food and a picture-perfect little infinity swimming pool in the lovely landscaped gardens.

Queen's Hotel

4 Dalada Veediya, Kandy; tel: 081-223 3026; www.queenshotel.lk; $$

This venerable hotel is worth staying at for its location, right opposite the Temple of the Tooth, and for its nostalgic value. Rooms are a bit creaky and road noise can be a problem, although rates are excellent value.

Get a round in   *Chic decor is a hallmark of Heritance hotels*

Sharon Inn

59 Saranankara Road; tel: 081 220 1400; www.hotelsharoninn.com; $$

Neat, modern and very professionally run guesthouse with comfortable rooms, excellent food and superb views over the lake and town from its hillside setting.

Hill Country: Nuwara Eliya

Glendower

5 Grand Hotel Road, Nuwara Eliya; tel: 052-222 2501; www.hotelglendower.com; $$$$

Small and extremely cosy faux-colonial bungalow hotel in a leafy setting by the golf course. Its nine rooms have polished wooden floors and furniture, and beds with plenty of blankets and quilts. The breakfast room transforms into the King Prawn Chinese restaurant for lunch and dinner, and there's a welcoming pub plus a roaring log fire in the lounge.

The Grand

Grand Hotel Road, Nuwara Eliya; tel: 052-222 2881; www.tangerinehotels.com; $$$$

This huge old colonial hotel is one of Nuwara Eliya's major landmarks. The imposing exterior and time-warped public areas are a superb reminder of Victorian times, although the rooms themselves disappointingly ordinary, and expensive at current rates.

Heritance Tea Factory

Kandapola, Nuwara Eliya; tel: 052-555 5000; www.heritancehotels.com; $$$

One of Sri Lanka's most ingenious hotels, occupying a converted tea factory – the exterior has been perfectly preserved but the interior magically transformed into a sleek, modern five-star hotel, combining futuristic architectural lines with lots of old tea-making memorabilia. The amazing setting is another major draw, high up in one of the most spectacular parts of the Nuwara Eliya region and surrounded by miles of tea plantations.

Hill Club

29 Grand Hotel Road, Nuwara Eliya; tel: 052-222 2653; www.hillclubsrilanka.net; $$$$

Set in a 1930s mock-Gothic building close to the town centre, this famous colonial hotel offers a real taste of the Ceylon of yesteryear. Mobile phones and children under 16 are banned, and the interior reeks of nostalgia, with a musty library, casual and residents' bars plus assorted stuffed stags' heads and cracked leather furniture. Accommodation is in neat, slightly chintzy rooms with creaking wood floors.

St Andrew's

10 St Andrew's Drive, Nuwara Eliya; tel: 052-222 3031; www.jetwinghotels.com; $$$$

Nuwara Eliya's smartest hotel, occupying a beautiful colonial country club surrounded by graceful lawns running

A four-poster bed at the Fortress

down to the golf course. The oak-panelled bar and restaurant are pure Edwardian period pieces, while rooms are cosy and comfortable.

The Planter's Bungalow

Wellawaya Rd; tel: 057 492 5902, www.plantersbungalow.com; $$$

Set in a gorgeous rural location 10km (6.2 miles) south of Ella, Planter's Bungalow offers a winning combination of contemporary comfort with a dash of colonial style. Accommodation is in three stylish rooms in the main building – a superbly restored nineteenth-century tea planter's bungalow – plus one cottage in the garden outside, and there's also authentic hill country-style Sri Lankan food, including enormous breakfasts. Room rates are remarkably low given the quality.

Waterfalls Homestay

Kithalella; tel: 057 567 6933; www.waterfalls-guesthouse-ella.com; $$

As the name suggests, this place is more like a homestay than a conventional guest house, tucked away just outside Ella village in an idyllic location facing Little Rawana Ella Falls. The atmosphere is very peaceful and intimate, with just three rooms (including one triple/family room), comfortably and colourfully furnished, and communal meals served in the kitchen-cum-dining room or on the lovely terrace outside.

Cultural Triangle: Habarana

Habarana Village By Cinnamon

Habarana; tel: 066-227 0047; www.cinnamonhotels.com; $$$$

This shares an entrance drive with its neighbour Cinnamon Lodge and is run by the same company, but there the similarity ends. This resort (formerly known as Chaaya Village), popular with package tourists, is sprawled across luxuriant land bordering a stunning lake, with accommodation in village-style chalets, offering comfort and convenience. A triangular swimming pool with three levels that seems to taper off into the jungle is a bonus. It is an informal place to stay, with all meals served as buffets and an open-sided bar, plus the delightful Asmara Indonesian spa and a jogging track.

Cinnamon Lodge

Habarana; tel: 066-227 0011; www.cinnamonhotels.com; $$$$

Set in a forested park around Habarana lake, this resort's rooms are built as local-style villas with either a veranda or balcony and intriguing, Kandyan-style interiors with arches, alcoves and valances. Watch out for inquisitive monkeys when walking in the grounds, and large squirrels begging for bread at breakfast.

Cultural Triangle: Giritale

The Deer Park Hotel

Giritale; tel: 027 224 6272, www.deerparksrilanka.com; $$$$

Night falls on the Fortress   *The infinity pool at Heritance Kandlama*

Tranquil eco-resort discretely buried away amidst tropical jungle close to the Minneriya National Park. Accommodation is in stylish individual chalets dotted around beautiful wooded grounds, and there's also a nice pool and Ayurveda centre.

Cultural Triangle: Dambulla

Heritance Kandalama
Kandalama, Dambulla;
tel: 066-555 5000; www.heritance
hotels.com; $$$$

One of Sri Lanka's most original hotels, this Bawa-designed establishment offers the ultimate marriage of architecture and nature, clinging to the side of a rocky outcrop and almost completely buried by layers of tropical vegetation. Stunning views of Sigiriya and the Kandalama lake, plush modern rooms, and one of the island's most spectacular swimming pools all add to the allure.

Cultural Triangle: Sigiriya

Elephant Corridor Hotel
Kibissa; tel: 066 228 6950;
www.elephantcorridor.com; $$$$

Very exclusive boutique hotel sprawling across 80 hectares (200 acres) of unfenced natural scrubland with superb views of nearby Sigiriya. The 21 luxurious suites come with private plunge pools and every imaginable mod con and there's also an alluring spa, although the whole place comes with a very hefty price tag.

Jetwing Vil Uyana
Tel: 066 492 3585; www.jetwinghotels.
com; $$$$

The Cultural Triangle's most memorable place to stay – and a remarkable experiment in eco-friendly tourist development. Vil Uyana occupies a large tract of reclaimed agricultural land which has been turned into a mixed habitat comprising sections of marsh, paddy, forest and lake, with expansive wetlands created using traditional Sri Lankan irrigation techniques – a marvellous oasis, wonderfully tranquil and rich in birdlife and other natural attractions. Accommodation is in individual chalets modelled on traditional Sinhalese village architecture but luxuriously appointed inside with all mod-cons, while the main building, with restaurant, bar, spa and library, is contemporary Sri Lankan design at its most stunning.

East Coast: Trincomalee

Trinco Blu by Cinnamon
Sampaltivu Post, Uppuveli; tel: 011-230 660; www.cinnamonhotels.com; $$$$

This sprawling five-star resort hotel (formerly known as the Chaaya Blu) is the major landmark along the coast north of Trincomalee. Recently refurbished, it now offers stylish rooms, a good spread of facilities and a fine stretch of unspoilt beach, although rates are steep. Also has a dive school and is a good place to arrange whale-watching trips even if you're not staying here.

The Bawa-designed Heritance Kandalama

Welcombe Hotel

66 Lower Road, Orr's Hill, Trincomalee; tel: 026-222 3886; www.welcombehotel.com; $$

Built in the 1930s, this hotel has undergone several changes over the years – from Trincomalee's favourite hostelry to being taken over by the army in the 1990s. The quirky modern building, topped with recycled railway sleepers, is attractive, and rooms are spacious and comfortable. The 1930s wood-panelled bar remains intact, as does the spirit of polite hospitality. Its position at the top of a very steep hill commands the finest views over Trincomalee's harbour. The restaurant offers seafood, Oriental, European and Sri Lankan cuisines.

South Coast: Galle

Amangalla

10 Church Street, Fort; 091-222 3388; www.amanresorts.com; $$$$

Occupying the sensitively restored premises of Galle's famous old New Oriental Hotel, this establishment remains wonderfully faithful to the period character of its colonial predecessor, combining old-world colonial chic with the last word in contemporary luxury – a compelling combination, though at a considerable price.

Fortaleza

9 Church Cross Street, Galle Fort; 091 223 3415; www.fortaleza.lk; $$$

The original Fortaleza was once a spice warehouse, built around 1700 in the heart of Galle Fort. Now it is renovated and converted into a boutique hotel, restaurant and bar. Comprises of 16 separate and comfortable bedrooms.

The Fort Printers

39 Pedlar Street, Galle Fort; tel: 091 224 7977; www.thefortprinters.com; $$$$

Characterful boutique hotel in the very heart of old Galle, occupying the barn-like building which formerly housed the town's printing shop. The hotel's five suites are little museum-pieces of Dutch colonial architecture, with creaking wooden floors and high beamed ceilings, the rather austere effect relieved by a generous dash of colourful fabrics and artworks.

Galle Fort Hotel

28 Church Street, Fort; tel: 091-223 2870; www.galleforthotel.com; $$$$

Stunning hotel set in a magnificently converted old Dutch warehouse – like the nearby Amangalla, it manages to combine colonial charm and contemporary luxury, though at a far more affordable price. It also dishes up some of Sri Lanka's best foreign cuisine, with a predominantly Southeast Asian slant – a pleasant change if you have had one too many rice and curries.

Jetwing Lighthouse

Dadella, Galle; tel: 091-222 3744; www.jetwinghotels.com; $$$$

The Fortress's pool   *Buffet dining at Habarana Village*

Set on a breezy stretch of seafront a couple of kilometres outside Galle, this Geoffrey Bawa-designed hotel is one of the great Sri Lankan architect's defining creations, with a simple, serene exterior, gorgeously designed rooms and splashes of local colour (such as the remarkable quirky wrought-iron staircase depicting the Portuguese arrival in Sri Lanka). Excellent food and heaps of facilities too, as well as intriguing activities such as cooking lessons with the hotel's head chef, which is highly recommended.

Kahanda Kanda

Angulugaha, Galle; tel: 091-494 3700; www.kahandakanda.com; $$$$

For a touch of complete luxury, the KK offers the feel of staying in a private villa with all the amenities of a 5-star hotel. There are just eight suites, all uniquely decorated and located in their own buildings, with stunning views over the surrounding jungle and tea plantations. Relax in the garden, swim in the infinity pool, enjoy a massage or learn how to cook Sri Lankan dishes.

The Sun House

18 Upper Dickson Road, Galle; tel: 091-438 0275; www.thesun house.com; $$$$

This long-established boutique guesthouse is still one of the nicest places to stay in Sri Lanka, set in a beautiful old 19th-century planter's villa on a hill high above Galle, with oodles of period charm and memorable cooking. The adjacent Dutch House offers a slightly more upmarket variation on the same theme, with four huge suites in another historic colonial mansion.

South Coast: Koggala

The Fortress

Koggala; tel: 091 438 9400, www.thefortress.lk; $$$$

One of the south's most luxurious and expensive hotels, this striking five-star resort is designed to resemble a supersized version of one of Galle's old colonial-era Dutch villas, magnificently framed between superbly landscaped grounds, a vast infinity pool and the sea. The opulent rooms boast all mod-cons, while facilities include a top-notch spa and several excellent restaurants.

South Coast: Yala

Cinnamon Wild Yala

Kirinda, Tissamaharama; tel: 011-230-6600; www.cinnamonhotels.com; $$$$

Over 50 chalets with jungle-themed decor are set in a huge, unfenced area at the borders of the Yala National Park where wild animals roam. Chalets have composition roof, particle board ceilings and mock-timber furniture to complement the surrounding wilderness without plundering it. Perfect tranquillity in a conserved natural setting by beach and lake.

Egg hoppers and characteristic spices

RESTAURANTS

Colombo

Bay Leaf

79 Gregory's Road, Colombo 7; tel: 011-269 5920; daily 11am–11pm; $$$
Upmarket Italian restaurant in a sedate old colonial villa in the diplomats' district of Colombo. The menu features a good selection of home-made pastas, pizzas – and there's a nice little bar with excellent cocktails.

Chesa Swiss

3 Deal Place A, Colombo 3: tel: 011-257 3433; Mon–Sat noon–2.30 & 7–10.30pm, Sat 7–10.30pm; $$$$
One of the smartest restaurants in Colombo, set in a charming colonial villa and offering a sumptuously prepared range of Swiss food, Australian steaks, seafood and vegetarian dishes.

Chutneys

Cinnamon Grand hotel, Galle Road, Colombo 3; tel: 011 249 7372; daily 7pm to midnight; $$$
Chic South Indian restaurant with a very original twist, serving up little-known

Price guide for a two-course meal for one:
$$$$ = over Rs3000
$$$ = Rs1500–3000
$$ = Rs750–1500
$ = below Rs750

regional dishes and street food from India's four southernmost states – Kerala, Tamil Nadu, Andhra Pradesh and Karnataka. There's a particularly good vegetarian selection, plus meat and seafood mains, all bursting with chilli, tamarind and coconut flavours, served up on traditional metal plates and accompanied by authentically fiery chutneys. Excellent value. Open evenings only.

Cricket Club Café

34 Queens Road (off Duplication Road); tel: 011-250 1384; www.thecricketclubcafe ceylon.com; daily 11am–11pm; $$$
Eternally popular cricket-themed bar-café-restaurant in an old colonial villa. Watch videos of famous matches and ogle the memorabilia plastered all over the walls whilst tucking into one of the café's well-prepared international standards – burgers, sandwiches, pasta dishes and the like.

Gallery Cafe

2 Alfred House Road, off Alfred House Gardens; tel: 011-258 2162, www.paradise road.lk/gallery_cafe; daily 10am–11.30pm; $$$$
Colombo's smartest café, and definitely one of the places to be seen, with a good range of international cuisine and what are claimed to be the capital's best desserts – although service can be

Dinner on the terrace   *Mount Lavinia's Seafood Cove*

distinctly hit or miss. Or just come for a drink and the chance to watch Colombo's smart set at play

Green Cabin
453 Galle Road, Colombo 3; tel: 011-228 8811; daily 11am–3pm, 6–11pm; $
Excellent little Sri Lankan café, long established and patronised mainly by locals, but an ideal place to test-drive the local cuisine at low prices including lamprais, and hoppers and curry.

London Grill
Cinnamon Grand, 77 Galle Road, Colombo 3; tel: 011-249 7379; www.cinnamonhotels.com; daily 7–11pm $$$$
In the basement of the Cinnamon Grand Hotel, this restaurant is the genuine thing: an unreconstructed 1970s steakhouse, with original plush decor and banquette seating. The menu runs the full gamut of steaks, grills, game and seafood, and the sensational preparations are matched by courteous and efficient service.

Long Feng
Cinnamon Lakeside Hotel, 115 Sir Chittampalam A. Gardiner Mawatha, Colombo 2; tel: 011 249 1949; daily noon–3pm, 7pm–11pm; $$$
One of the city's top Chinese restaurants, this classy establishment specialises in authentic Sichuan cooking, with a few more mainstream Cantonese dishes too.

Navratna
Taj Samudra hotel, 25 Galle Face Centre Road, Colombo 3; tel: 011 244 6622; daily 12.30–3pm, 7–11pm; $$$$
Arguably Sri Lanka's best Indian restaurant, specialising in unusual regional specialities from around the subcontinent.

Palmyrah Restaurant
Renuka Hotel, 328 Galle Road; tel: 011-257 3598; daily noon–2.30pm, 7–10.30pm; $$
Cosy but unpretentious basement restaurant serving up one of the city's best selections of traditional Sri Lankan cuisine including authentic curries, hoppers, pitta and kottu rotty. Also offers a rare chance to sample northern Sri Lankan-style dishes from the city of Jaffna, full of rich, feisty spices.

Royal Thai
Cinnamon Lakeside, 115 Sir Chittampalam A. Gardiner Mawatha, Colombo 2; tel: 011-249 1945; www.cinnamonhotels.com; daily noon–3pm, 7–11pm; $$$
This lavish Thai restaurant overlooks the hotel's garden, pool and lake, with exquisite decor matched by staff in traditional Thai costumes. The menu has an excellent selection of fiery dishes, including standards like green and red curries, pad thai and more unusual regional specialities. Reservations usually essential, even for lunch.

Semondu
Dutch Hospital, Bank of Ceylon Mawatha opposite the World Trade Centre; tel: 011-

In Royal Thai

244 1590, www.semondu.com; daily noon–2.30pm, 7–11pm; $$–$$$$

This beautiful restaurant in the atmospheric old Dutch Hospital is the brainchild of Sri Lankan Airlines, offering its own brand of 'fusion from the skies' featuring a well-prepared selection of upmarket international mains, often with a Sri Lankan or Oriental twist. The express lunch is a particularly good deal.

Tao

Cinnamon Grand Hotel, 77 Galle Rd, Colombo 3; tel: 011 249 7369; daily 7–11pm; $$$$

Set in the gardens of the Cinnamon Grand, whose trees twinkle with fairy lights after dark, Tao dishes up fine fusion cuisine blending Sri Lankan traditions with Asian and European influences. Mains range from seafood and meat standards to more innovative creations, like the combination plate of red curry chicken, grilled lamb chops and spiced tiger prawns.

West Coast: Negombo

King Coconut

11 Porutota Road; tel: 031-227 8043; daily 11am–11pm; $$

Lively beachside restaurant known for its relaxed atmosphere and big selection of fresh seafood, plus tasty rice and curry thalis at affordable prices. Free WiFi available.

Tuskers

83 Ethukala Road; tel: 031 222 6999; daily

10am–10pm; $$$

Smart restaurant in an attractive open-sided pavilion just off the main tourist drag (but carefully screened from it). The menu focuses on a small but excellently prepared range of mainly European-style meat and fish dishes (and pasta) along with a few Sri Lankan- and Chinese-style mains.

West Coast: Bentota

Club Villa

138/15 Galle Road, southern end of Bentota; tel: 034-227 5312; $$$

Even if you're not staying here, it's worth visiting this excellent little hotel for a chance to soak up the atmosphere and savour the well-prepared and very modestly priced international cuisine in the beautiful garden restaurant.

Golden Grill

National Tourist Resort, Bentota; tel: 034-227 5455; daily 10am–10pm: $$

A local institution, the Golden Grill has been open for 30 years with a dependable menu which has hardly changed that whole time. The mixed grill with beef, chicken, pork, sausage, bacon, egg, three different vegetables, French fries and salad is the island's best and curries (from mild to hot) are always available. Other specialities are fresh fish including shark, and flaming dishes, whether steak or the pineapple surprise dessert.

Lunuganga

Dedduwa Lake; tel: 091 428 7056;

Fresh chillis for heat

www.lunuganga.com; daily 9am–5pm;
$$$$

The bumpy 5km (3-mile) ride off the main road in Bentota to reach Lunuganga is well worth the effort to experience the island's most magical garden retreat, the spiritual home and country estate of renowned architect, Geoffrey Bawa. Cuisine focuses on the sort of Sri Lankan home cooking that Bawa himself enjoyed, using fresh, seasonal ingredients. Reservations are obligatory.

Malli's
Opposite The Surf hotel; tel: 0778 514 894;
$$$$

Hidden upstairs above a line of shops by the railway tracks, this unexpectedly upmarket little restaurant specializes in sophisticated Sri Lankan and Asian-style seafood and other creations (including good rice and curry) with a hint of fusion inventiveness – think panfried mahi-mahi with rösti and saffron sauce, for example.

West Coast: Hikkaduwa

Asian Jewel
Baddegama Road; tel: 091 493 1388;
www.asian-jewel.com/asian-jewel.html;
daily until 9pm; $$$

Eclectic but excellently prepared range of Western or Asian cuisine, travelling the spectrum from full English breakfasts to Thai chicken curry and Indian specialities, as well as the standard rice and curry – or preorder the house speciality, shepherd's pie. Book in advance.

Spaghetti & Co
644 Galle Road; tel: 091 227 7042;
Thiranagama; daily 6–10.30pm; $$

Soothing Italian-owned garden restaurant offering up some of Sri Lanka's best pizza and pasta at very reasonable prices.

East Coast: Trincomalee

Welcombe Hotel
66 Lower Rd, Orr's Hill; tel: 026 222 2373;
daily 6am–10pm; $$

The smartest restaurant in Trinco (although still relatively inexpensive), serving up a mix of the usual Sri Lankan standards plus a few European mains. Sit either on the beautiful outdoor terrace high above the Inner Harbour or the dining room inside.

Cultural Triangle: Around Kandy

The Pub
36 Dalada Veediya; tel: 081-232 4868; daily 11am–1am (bar closed 2–5pm); $$$

Drawing in a largely tourist crowd, The Pub makes a nice change from rice and curry, with a decent spread of European classics – anything from spaghetti carbonara to pork chops. The balcony is a good place to have a beer and watch the hustle and bustle of Dalada Vidiya below.

Sharon Inn
59 Saranankara Rd; tel: 081 222 2416; daily 7.30–10pm; $$$

The nightly rice and curry buffet (daily at 7.30pm) at the Sharon Inn guesthouse

A tasty biryani

is one of the best in the island, featuring a fine spread of fifteen or so dishes with the emphasis on unusual local vegetables which you'll not have tasted before. Non-guests should reserve in advance by 4pm at the latest.

The White House

21 Dalada Vidiya; tel: 081 223 2765; daily noon–10pm; $$$

Long-established restaurant, recently given a thorough upgrade and makeover. Downstairs there's now a chic modern bakery with assorted cakes and short eats, plus rice and curry lunchtime buffets. Upstairs, a rather sedate dining room features a mix of Sri Lankan, Indian and Chinese mains along with pasta, seafood and steaks. Unlicensed.

Cultural Triangle: Habarana

Ehala Restaurant

Cinnamon Lodge, Habarana; tel: 066-227 0011; www.cinnamonhotels.com; daily 6.30–10am, 12.30–2.30pm, 7.30–10pm; $$$

Overlooking the swimming pool of the Cinnamon Lodge hotel, this attractive open-air restaurant serves lavish international buffets. Alternatively, the hotel's The Lotus restaurant offers a more upmarket dining experience, specialising in 'organic fine dining' with produce delivered daily from the hotel's own local farm.

Hill Country

Bandarawela Hotel

14 Welimada Road, Bandarawela; tel: 057-222 2501; www.aitkenspencehotels.com/bandarawelahotel; daily 12.30am–2.30pm, 7.30–10pm; $$

Stately old colonial-style dining room offering local and international cuisine, along with lighter snacks and sandwiches. Alternatively, just take morning or afternoon tea on the spacious front lawn.

The Hill Club

29 Grand Hotel Drive, Nuwara Eliya; tel: 052 222 2653; daily 6–11pm; $$$$

The famous dinners here offer a real taste of the colonial life of yesteryear. The food itself is average, but the time-warped atmosphere, with dinner served promptly at 8pm by white-gloved waiters in the chintzy dining room, is strangely romantic, if decidedly formal – men are only admitted if clad in the obligatory jacket and tie (available free on loan at the club if you don't have your own).

Railway Carriage Restaurant TCK 6685

Heritance Tea Factory Hotel, Kandapola, Nuwara Eliya; tel: 052-555 5000; www.heritancehotels.com/teafactory; daily 7.30–10.30pm; $$$

Quirky but classy fine-dining restaurant, located in a restored narrow-gauge railway carriage. Food features top-quality global ingredients – Norwegian salmon, Australian lamb from Australia and so on, backed up with vegetables from the hotel's own organic allotment and an international wine list – all showcased in the restaurant's signature six-course (or

All aboard the TCK 6685   *A fine rice and curry spread*

'six station') menu. With only 16 seats, booking is essential.

South Coast: Unawatuna

Kingfisher

Devala Road, Unawatuna, Galle; tel: 94 912 250 312; www.kingfisherunawatuna.com; daily 7.30am–midnight; $$

The best of the many informal café-restaurants lined up along Unawatuna Beach, with beautiful views of the waves from its neat little terrace. Recently refurbished, the restaurant serves wraps, pasta, salads, Thai curries and seafood straight from the Indian Ocean, including lobster. A hypnotic chill-out soundtrack and wide range of drinks rounds things off.

Thaproban Beach House

Yaddhehimulla Road; tel: 091 438 1722; daily 7.30am–10.30pm; $$.

Unawatuna's smartest and liveliest restaurant offers consistently good cooking including fresh seafood, above-average pizzas, rice and curry and a smattering of international dishes. Service comes with a smile and prices are very reasonable.

South Coast: Galle

Amangalla

10 Church Street; tel: 091-239 3388, www.amanresorts.com/amangalla/home. aspx; daily 7.30am–11pm; $$$$

The gracious old colonial-style dining room at the superb Amangalla hotel is one of the most memorable places to eat in the south. Delicious light meals are rustled up for lunch, while dinner features a mix of top-notch Sri Lankan and international cuisine. Alternatively (and less expensively), come for a superior high tea on the hotel's open verandah.

Apa Villa Illuketia

Thalpe, near Galle; tel: 091 228 3320; www.villa-srilanka.com/apailluketia; $$$

One of the few private villas (owned by the founder of Insight Guides) to open its doors to non-resident dinner guests. The three-course rice and curry dinner prepared with organically grown vegetables and red rice from their own grounds has a reputation that extends beyond Galle, and the lemon grass soup is to die for. Reservations are a must.

Mama's Galle Fort Rooftop Café

76 Leyn Baan Street; tel: 091-222 6415; www.mamas-galle-fort.com; $$

This quaint, down-to-earth rooftop eatery, part of a popular guest house in the heart of Galle Fort, is a breezy stop for rice and curry lunches, ideal on humid days. Service is slow when they get busy.

Wijaya Beach Restaurant

Dalawela, Galle; tel: 091 228 3610; daily 8.30am–11pm; $$$

This cool beachfront restaurant is a particular favourite with the Galle expat set and usually gets packed out from lunchtime onwards. Food includes excellent wood-fired pizzas, plus daily specials, wraps and home made puddings and there's a good drinks list including cocktails, wine and Sol beer.

Buddha at the Seema Malakaya, Colombo

A–Z

A

Admission charges

Entry fees to state-sponsored institutions like museums, the zoo and the elephant orphanage are based on a two-tier system: tourists pay up to 20 times more than Sri Lankans or foreigners with resident visas. Fees are quoted in US dollars but payable in Sri Lanka rupees.

There is officially no charge at many temples, although some of the most prominent places – most notably Kandy's Temple of the Tooth and the Dambulla Cave Temples – do levy an entrance fee.

Entrance charges for foreigners have skyrocketed in recent years. Sites in the Cultural Triangle are particularly expensive – $25 at Polonnaruwa and Anuradhapura, and $30 at Sigiriya, for example. Other notable attractions such as the Pinnewala Elephant Orphanage and Colombo Zoo also levy relatively hefty entrance charges, particularly when compared with what locals pay to get in.

Age restrictions

To qualify for reduced entry charges, children need to be under 12. To drive you must be over 18; to drink and go to casinos, at least 18.

B

Begging

Begging is far less common than in neighbouring India; most beggars will be seen congregating by the entrance to temples, churches or tourist attractions. As many of these are clearly elderly, infirm or disabled, it is fair to follow the example of the Sri Lankans, who believe to give is to earn merit and will spare a coin to those they see as genuine beggars. Some beggars deliberately target tourists – donations to a suitable charity may ultimately prove more effective. Opportunistic requests by passing children (and occasionally even adults) for 'one pen', 'one sweet' or, increasingly, just 'money' are also common.

Budgeting

It's still possible to find double rooms in a simple guesthouses for around Rs2000 a night (although most places cost considerably more), and to eat in basic cafés for Rs1,000 a day (although again, expect to pay double that in more touristy establishments). Realistically, however, you'll be looking at a minimum of around $40–50 per day per person in order to guarantee comfortable lodgings and decent food (and drink), while the sky's the limit if you wish to sample

Sri Lankan flag

the island's more luxurious hotels and hire your own transport.

C

Carbon offsetting

Air travel produces a huge amount of carbon dioxide and is a significant contributor to global warming. If you would like to offset the damage caused to the environment by your flight, a number of organisations do this, using online 'carbon calculators', which tell you how much you need to donate. In the UK travellers can visit www.climatecare.org or www.carbonneutral.com; in the US log on to www.climatefriendly.com or www.sustainabletravelinternational.org.

Children

Sri Lankans adore children and make a great deal of fuss over them, and children happily enjoy the country's beaches, wildlife and exotic sights. Baby food and nappies are available in major supermarkets but are expensive.

Clothing

Cottons and light natural fabrics such as linen are ideal in the lowland heat. Skimpy skirts and brief shorts are not considered respectable (except in tourist hotels and adjacent beach areas), and will attract stares and a certain amount of hassle. For women, loose cotton skirts or trousers and tops, and a long dress or skirt and long-sleeved blouse for visiting temples are ideal.

Men will feel comfortable in cotton trousers or shorts and a T-shirt. For climate details, see page 12.

Crime and safety

Despite the end of the civil war, the political situation in Sri Lanka remains potentially volatile, and it's always worth checking the current situation before travelling to the north. There is an underlying threat from terrorism, although these days, international warnings regarding visiting Sri Lanka are considerably lesser than many parts of the world. While significantly reduced since the end of the conflict, security forces maintain a visible presence, particularly in the north and eastern provinces.

Apart from that, Sri Lanka is a reassuringly safe country. Levels of petty crime are far lower than in many other Asian countries, and violent attacks against tourists are relatively infrequent. Nevertheless, it pays to exercise caution and obey common-sense rules. Never flash valuables or leave them lying around; do not let your credit card out of your sight when making payments; avoid dark and deserted beaches at night; and do not accept lifts from strangers.

The most obvious safety hazard in Sri Lanka is traffic: the island has an abysmal record of road-related accidents and you should always stay alert when there's traffic around – vehicles often behave in unexpected and potentially dangerous ways. If you're cycling, take extra care.

A cow investigates some curd

Swimming is another potential hazard. Dozens of locals and the occasional tourist are drowned every year. If swimming off an unfrequented beach, always check local advice and make sure someone knows you're in the water. And never swim under the influence of alcohol.

Drugs are a problem in some coastal areas. Do not get tangled up in buying/ selling/using them or get involved with those who do: it is illegal and dangerous.

The following websites publish up-to-date travel advisories: www.gov.uk/foreign-travel-advice, www.travel.state.gov, and www.smartraveller.gov.au.

Customs

If you are bringing in over US$15,000 in cash or traveller's cheques, or valuable gems and jewellery, this should be declared at customs on arrival, to avoid problems when leaving. Duty-free allowances permit up to 1.5 litres of spirits, 2 bottles of wine, and perfume in a quantity for personal use. Note that you are not allowed to bring duty-free cigarettes into the country. Drugs are illegal, and possession could carry the death penalty.

On departure

Customs officers may check your luggage for items being taken out of the country without a permit. The export of 'antiques' (defined as anything over 50 years old) is prohibited without a special licence, as is the export of native fauna and flora.

Unused Sri Lankan currency should be reconverted into foreign currency (for-eign-exchange transaction receipts to prove you acquired Sri Lankan currency with foreign currency are technically required, but are almost never asked for).

D

Disabled travellers

Sri Lanka is not well equipped for those with physical disabilities. Only a few of the five-star hotels have access and facilities for people in wheelchairs – public transport has none. Wheelchairs are available at the international airport on prior request through the airlines.

E

Electricity

Sri Lanka uses 230–240 volts, 50 cycles, alternating current. Most sockets are three-pronged, usually with round pins, occasionally with UK-style square pins; adaptors are cheap and readily available from hardware shops. Power often fluctuates, even in the cities.

Embassies and high commissions

Australia. Australian High Commission; 21 Gregory's Road, Colombo 7, tel: 011-246 3200; www.srilanka.embassy.gov.au

Canada. High Commission of Canada; 33A 5th Lane, Colombo 3, tel: 011-532 6232; www.canadainternational.gc.ca/sri_lanka

New Zealand. New Zealand High Commission, New Delhi, India, is accredited

Stilt fishermen   *Mural in Anuradhapura*

to Sri Lanka; www.nzembassy.com
South Africa. South African High Commission; 114 Rosmead Place, Colombo 7, tel: 011-246 3000

UK. British High Commission; 389 Bauddhaloka Mawatha, Colombo 7, tel: 011-539 0639; www.uk-embassy.net sri-lanka

USA. Embassy of the United States; 210 Galle Road, Colombo 3, tel: 011-249 8500; http://srilanka.usembassy.gov

Emergencies

Fire and Ambulance: 110
Police: 119 (in Colombo), 118 (elsewhere on the island)
Tourist Police: Anuradhapura 025-222 4546; Bentota 034-227 5022; Colombo 011-242 1451; Hikkaduwa 091-227 7222; Polonnaruwa 027-222 3099

Etiquette

Few Sri Lankans use cutlery, most picking up food with their hands, although visitors may feel more comfortable using a spoon and fork. However, food should be handled with the right hand only, as the left is considered unclean. When handing objects to another person, either the right hand or both hands should be used.

Away from the beach, wearing torn T-shirts, skimpy skirts, transparent clothing or displaying bare shoulders is considered highly improper, especially in temples, religious sites or in the presence of monks. When entering holy areas, it is customary to remove your shoes and walk barefoot within the designated area.

(This also applies to people's homes.) Women should wear long skirts or loose trousers and a modest blouse, or a loose cotton dress. Men should wear long trousers. Even ancient ruined temples in archaeological sites are still considered sacred, and should be treated as such.

Public displays of physical affection should be avoided.

When invited to a home, it is customary to bring fruit, tea or biscuits or some other small gift. Small presents from one's home country are very much appreciated.

Courtesy is an inherent part of Sri Lankan culture, and one which you should reciprocate. The loss of temper and raising of voices will cause offence, and is very unlikely to further your cause, whatever it is. Many Sri Lankans habitually ask personal questions of all foreigners they meet: you will regularly be asked your country, possibly followed by your age, marital status and number of children. Although such questioning by strangers might be considered intrusive in Western societies, in Sri Lanka these are ordinary questions and simply reflect the emphasis locals place on family life. You may also find yourself being stared at every now and then – not something that's considered rude in the same way as it is in the West.

Waggling the head from side to side is not a negative gesture but a slightly ambiguous gesture meaning either yes, or at least that the matter is being considered.

National Day festivities in Negombo

G

Gay and lesbian travellers

Homosexuality is illegal in Sri Lanka, so discretion is advised.

Green issues

There is a burgeoning awareness of green issues in the country, particularly when it comes to the tourist industry, with government authorities keen to promote the island's ecological credentials – although cynics might argue that this has more to do with cashing in on a potentially lucrative subsection of the tourist trade rather than with real actions on the ground. Nevertheless, eco-awareness increasingly extends to many parts of the island, with hotel chains, tour operators, tea plantations and so on all keen to establish their environmental credentials through a range of initiatives including recycling, organic farming, water-harvesting and so on.

H

Health

Inoculations

Proof of immunisation is not normally required, unless you have passed through an infected area within 14 days prior to your arrival. It is, however, advisable to ensure your immunisations for diphtheria, tetanus, hepatitis A and polio are topped up.

Be aware that all regions of Sri Lanka experience outbreaks of the mosquito-born dengue fever. During the first part of 2015, over 15,000 suspected dengue fever cases were reported. Almost half of them occurred in Western Province, where Colombo lies.

Healthcare and insurance

The Sri Lankan health service does not provide free treatment for visitors, so your own insurance is vital.

Hospitals

Private doctors and good private hospitals are to be found in Colombo and tourist areas. The medical care at Colombo's private hospitals, centred around Nugegoda, is excellent and inexpensive, if a little informal (visitors are allowed at any time), and some tourists visit Sri Lanka specifically for medical treatment in private hospital rooms furnished like hotels. In Colombo, these include the **Apollo**, 578 Elvitigala Mawatha, Colombo 5, tel: 011-543 0000; the **Nawaloka**, 23 Sri Sugathodaya Mawatha, Colombo 2, tel: 011-254 4444, www.nawaloka.com; and **Oasis**, 18A M. E. D. Dabare Mawatha, Narahenpita, Colombo 5, tel: 011-550 6000, www.oasishospital.lk; in Galle, the **Ruhunu** Hospital, Karapitiya Road, tel: 091-223 4059.

Pharmacies

Most Western medicines are available, and so are many Indian substitutes. The Colombo branch of the state-run Osusala Pharmacy (255 Dharmapala

Sri Lankan banknotes

Mawatha/Lipton Circus, Colombo 7; tel: 011-269 4716) is open 24 hours and every town has several pharmacies.

Hours and holidays

Hours

Government offices, including post offices, and businesses observe a five-day working week, opening Monday to Friday from around 8.30 or 9.30am and closing around 4.30 or 5.30pm. Banks open Monday to Friday from 8 or 9am until 1 or 3pm; some branches also open on Saturday mornings. All shops and banks close on public holidays. Most branches of Keells and Cargills supermarkets are open 8am–8pm every day. In small towns, the shopping hours depend on the shop owner; many open late and on Sunday.

Public holidays

Public, bank and Poya (full moon) holidays change every year as they are based on lunar cycles. The constant national holidays are: 4 February – Independence Day; 1 May – May Day; 25 December – Christmas Day.

The Muslim holidays of Id-Ul-Fitr (Ramadan Festival Day), Id-Ul-Allah (Hajji Festival Day) and Milad-Un-Nabi (Holy Prophet's Birthday) are also national holidays celebrated on different days each year, according to the cycles of the Muslim calendar.

Other holidays usually occur in the following months:

January: Tamil Thai Pongal, Durutu Poya

February: Navan Poya
March: Mahasivarathri, Medin Poya
March/April: Good Friday
April: Day prior to Sinhalese/Tamil New Year, Sinhalese/Tamil New Year, Bak Poya
May: Vesak Poya and day after
June: Poson Poya
July: Esala Poya
August: Nikini Poya
September: Binara Poya
October: Vap Poya
October/November: Deepavali
November: Il Poya
December: Unduvap Poya

I

Internet

Internet cafés are widely found even in the smallest towns, with most places charging in the region off Rs75–150/hour. Increasing numbers of hotels, guesthouses and cafés are now offering Wi-fi (usually free to guests and customers).

L

Language

The main language is Sinhala, spoken by around 75 percent of the population. Tamil is the first language of around 25 percent, as both Tamils and east-coast Muslims speak it. English serves as the language of business and tourism and is spoken well by around 10 percent of the population, while many more can communicate adequately. Sinhala-speakers generally respond to

Policeman

foreigners' attempts to speak their language with incomprehension and prefer to practise their English instead. See page 116 for some helpful phrases in Sinhala and Tamil.

M

Maps

Useful for finding your way around Colombo and the major towns is Arjuna's A–Z Street Guide, available from Colombo bookshops. If you have any trouble with finding a place you would like to visit, contact the Tourism Hotline on tel: 1912 (only in Sri Lanka).

Media

Newspapers

Sri Lanka has three daily English newspapers and three Sunday newspapers with island-wide circulation; these are mainly available from stalls and pavement sellers. The *Daily News* (www.dailynews.lk) and the *Sunday Observer* (www.sundayobserver.lk) are state-controlled and thus serve as mouthpieces for the government. Independent newspapers include *The Island* and *Sunday Island* (www.island.lk), and the *Daily Mirror* (www.dailymirror.lk) and its sister publication the *Sunday Times* (www.sundaytimes.lk). While international magazines such as *Newsweek* and *Time* can be bought locally, foreign newspapers cannot. The free monthly magazine *Explore Sri Lanka* carries feature articles as well as information of interest to visitors.

Radio

There are several English-language radio stations churning out mainstream pop music and cheesy chat. The best is TNL Radio (101.7 FM; www.tnlrocks.com); others worth a listen are Yes FM (89.5 FM; www.yesfmonline.com) and Sun FM (99.9 FM).

Television

Sri Lankan television is unlikely to take up much of your time; both state and private channels broadcast mainly in Sinhala or Tamil, and what little English-language programming there is tends to be fairly dire. Satellite television is available island-wide with international news channels.

Money

Currency

The national currency is the Sri Lankan rupee. Coins come in denominations of one, two, five and 10 rupees, and notes in denominations of 10, 20, 50, 100, 500, 1,000, 2,000 and 5,000 rupees.

Credit cards

Most hotels, restaurants and shops accept credit cards. Visa and MasterCard are widely accepted; American Express and Diners Club less so. Be careful of credit card copying and don't allow your card out of your sight.

ATMs

There are hundreds of ATMs across the island that accept foreign Visa and/or

Pettah temple   *Post your letters here*

MasterCards; every town of any consequence will have at least one such machine where there is a bank.

Exchanging money

All banks change traveller's cheques, with Thomas Cook and American Express being the most widely recognised. The rate for traveller's cheques is better than for cash. Money can also be withdrawn on credit cards in banks, though it's generally easier and faster just to use an ATM (see above).

Tipping

Most hotels and restaurants add a 10 percent service charge to the bill, but you may wish to leave a tip if a service charge isn't included – and indeed even if it is, since there's no guarantee the additional service charge will find it's way to the person who actually served you. Chauffeurs and guides will also expect to be tipped somewhere in the region of US$5–10 per day, depending on their skills and helpfulness. Guides who show you around temples will expect a small tip (Rs100 should suffice, although do not give money directly to monks, but place it in a donation box).

P

Police

Sri Lankan police are generally friendly with foreigners, but if you have a problem or need to report a crime, it is best to take a Sinhala-speaking local with you. There are tourist police offices in a few towns, but these have little knowledge of tourism or tourists. If you have anything stolen and want to make an insurance claim, you will need a police report. The police uniform is khaki.

Post

When sending airmail letters or cards with stamps, make sure that they are franked in front of you at the post office counter. International courier services include the following:

DHL, 340 Galle Road, Colombo 3, tel: 011-438 4792

FedEx, 93 1/1 Chatham Street, Colombo 1, tel: 011-254 4357

R

Religion

There are four major religions in Sri Lanka: Buddhism (practised by roughly 70 percent of the population), Hinduism (15 percent), Christianity (7 percent) and Islam (7 percent). Almost all Sinhalese are Buddhist (there is a small number of Christian Sinhalese). The majority of Tamils are Hindu, though there are also significant numbers of Tamil Christians.

S

Smoking

The rules are confused but generally mean you can smoke when dining out

of doors, on a hotel's open-air terrace or in a restaurant's garden but, curiously, smoking is allowed in some hotel lounges if they have less than a specified number of guests, and in pubs, bars and casinos.

T

Telephones

There are several mobile-phone service providers; a local prepaid mobile-phone account can be set up easily.

The international dialling code to contact a number in Sri Lanka is 00 94. The first digit (0) of the phone numbers given in this guide should be omitted when telephoning from overseas. When telephoning someone in Colombo from a Colombo number, omit the 011 prefix.

Time Zone

Sri Lanka's clocks are set at Coordinated Universal Time UTC (GMT) +5.5 – in other words 5.5 hours ahead of GMT in winter, and 4.5 hours in summer. Sri Lanka is 4.5 hours behind Australia in winter and 5.5 hours in summer; or 10.5 hours ahead of New York in winter, and 9.5 in summer.

Toilets

Public toilets are virtually non-existent: in an emergency, head for the nearest hotel or decent pastry shop. It is prudent to carry a cache of toilet paper in case none is available.

Tourist information

The Sri Lanka Tourist Promotion Bureau has its own website with stacks of information (www.srilanka.travel). The head office is at 80 Galle Road, Colombo 3 (Mon–Fri 8.30am–4pm), tel: 011-242 6900, and there is a 24-hour counter in the arrivals hall (after customs) at the Colombo International Airport, tel: 011-225 2411, and in the Kandy City Centre mall (daily 8.30am–5pm), tel: 081-222 2661.

Overseas offices include:
UK. Sri Lanka Tourist Office, 1 Devonshire Square, London EC2M 4WD, tel: 0845-880 6333.

Transport

Airports – arrival and departure

Sri Lankan Airlines (airline code UL – or 'usually late' as the local joke goes) operates daily non-stop flights between Colombo and London Heathrow and some flights via the Maldives, as well as direct from Frankfurt, Paris and Rome. Other flights from Europe necessitate a change of planes in the Middle East. As well as UL, major airlines serving Colombo include British Airways, Cathay Pacific, Emirates, Etihad, Oman, Qatar, Royal Jordanian, Singapore and Thai. The airport is also served by regular charter flights from Europe.

Colombo International Airport is bright and usually functions smoothly; there are duty-free shops for arriving passengers after immigration. After

Negombo fishing vessels at sea

emerging from customs there is a lobby with banks (including an ATM), hotel and taxi counters. You can book a taxi to Colombo there for about Rs3000. Alternatively, free shuttle buses run every 30min to nearby Averiwatte bus station, from where onward buses run to Colombo, Kandy and Negombo, although it's a slow and crowded experience, and not great if you've just stepped off a long-haul flight.

On departure, porters are available and are worth it (Rs50 a bag) for getting you through the queues and luggage X-ray efficiently. Departure tax is included in the cost of your airline ticket.

Public transport

Bus. Buses reach pretty much every town or village of any significance anywhere on the island, though services are often slow, crowded and uncomfortable. Government buses (usually painted red or orange) are incredibly cheap but stop absolutely everywhere and usually get horribly packed – best avoided except for very short journeys. Private buses come in various standards and sizes – from big old rust buckets which are similar in speed, cost and comfort to government buses, ranging up through 'semi-express' and 'express' services, which tend to make fewer stops and thus reach destinations a bit faster. The fastest vehicles, called 'inter-city expresses', usually have air-conditioning, tinted windows and padded seats. These make only limited stops and don't accept standing passengers (at least in theory) and go pretty fast, sometimes recklessly so.

Train. Sri Lanka's antiquated railway system offers a charming – if slow – way of getting around the island, especially on the scenic hill-country line. Fares are low, though carriages can often get ridiculously overcrowded, and delays are the norm rather than the exception. There are three main lines starting from Colombo: the Coast Line runs north to Negombo and Puttalam and south to Galle and Matara (currently the line is being extended up to Beliatta, and there are plans to further extend it to Kataragama); the Main Line goes east, via Kandy, to Nanu Oya and Badulla; and the Northern Line goes via Anuradhapura to Vavuniya. A side branch of the Northern Line goes to Trincomalee, while another goes to Polonnaruwa and Batticaloa. For more information contact Train Enquiries on 011-242 1281 or visit www.railway. gov.lk.

Tuk-tuks and taxis

Tuk-tuks Motorised rickshaws (also known as tuk-tuks, trishaws, three-wheelers or just 'taxis') can be found everywhere in Sri Lanka and offer the most convenient way of making short journeys. They can also sometimes be useful for longer journeys in places which lack public transport. These noisy little vehicles can travel at surprising speed through busy traf-

Truck bearing a heavy load

fic, and offer a fun – if sometimes slightly nerve-wracking – way of getting around. Rickshaws aren't generally metered except in Colombo, where increasing numbers of metered vehicles can be found, currently charging Rs50/km. Assuming you're going in an unmetered rickshaw, you'll need to agree the fare before setting off, and be prepared to bargain. Rickshaw drivers vary enormously in how much they'll try to overcharge you by: many are fairly honest, though a few are complete rogues. You'll usually pay a bit more in big cities like Colombo and Kandy, and less in more rural areas; the more touristy the area you're in, the more you're likely to need to barter to get a reasonable fare. It's also a good idea to have the correct change for your journey, since rickshaw drivers often claim not to have any change, in the hope that you'll let them keep the difference.

Note that a proportion of hotels and guesthouses (and also some shops, spice gardens and restaurants) pay rickshaw drivers commission for bringing them business, meaning that certain drivers may attempt to steer you away from a place that doesn't pay commission to another place that does. Ignore any driver who tells you that your chosen hotel is full, has shut down, is derelict or teeming with rats – they may conceivably be telling the truth, but it's always a good idea to check for yourself. Remember too that if a hotel pays commission to a rickshaw driver, they'll most likely try to charge you a higher rate to compensate.

Taxis. As well as the ubiquitous motorised rickshaws (tuk-tuks), there are metered taxi services in Colombo, but they don't cruise or wait on the street like tuk-tuks and have to be booked by telephone. Some taxi firms with fixed rates per km: **Kangaroo Cabs**, tel: 011-2 588 588 and **GNTC**, tel: 011-268 8688. Away from the capital, 'taxis' are minivans; in most towns they congregate near bus stations waiting for custom, or can be arranged through your hotel.

Driving

Sri Lanka's anarchic traffic and idiosyncratic road rules make driving a challenge for foreigners. If you don't absolutely have to drive, the best option is to hire a car with a driver – which is often no more expensive than hiring a self-drive car. If you're determined to drive, you'll need an international driving licence, plus an additional permit (Rs1500, issued on the spot) from the Automobile Association of Ceylon (tel: 011-242 1528), 40 Sir Macan Markar Mawatha, just off Galle Face Green in Colombo.

Car Rental. Firms include **Quickshaws**, tel: 011 258 3133, www.quickshaws.com; **Casons Rent-A-Car**, tel: 011 440 5070; www.casonscar.com; **Mal-Key Rent-A-Car**, tel: 011-236 5251; www.malkey.lk.

Chauffeur-driven cars. Cars driven

Rail is a charming way to explore Sri Lanka

by chauffeur-guides can be arranged through your hotel, or you could get a quotation from a taxi company (see above) for an out-of-town tour.

V

Visas and passports

Nationals from all countries apart from the Maldives and Singapore now require a visa, or 'ETA' (Electronic Travel Authorization) to visit Sri Lanka. These can either be obtained online before you arrive at www.eta.gov.lk or on arrival at the airport. The fee for a tourist visa is currently $30 if bought in advance online ($15 for citzens of SAARC countries), or $35 if bought on arrival. The visa is valid for 30 days and for two entries. Passports must be valid for six months after arrival.

Visa extensions are given at the Immigration Service Centre (unit 01, Liberty Arcade Building, 282 R A De Mel Mawatha (Duplication Road), Colombo 3; tel: 011 237 5972; www.immigration.gov.lk). The charge is based on what your own country charges a visiting Sri Lankan (see the website for a complete list of fees). Conditions for extensions are an onward ticket and proof of sufficient funds to support oneself while in the country, calculated at US$15 a day (a credit card should suffice). Proof of money spent in the country may be required, so keep all traveller's cheque/ATM receipts. Extensions normally take an hour or two to process.

W

Websites

As well as the useful websites listed elsewhere in this book, the following may also be of interest:
www.srilanka.travel – Official website of the Sri Lanka Tourism Promotion Bureau.
www.lankalibrary.com – Eclectic treasure trove of weird and wonderful information about the island.
www.priu.gov.lk – Official website of the government of Sri Lanka.

Weights and measures

Sri Lanka uses the metric system; roads are marked in kilometres.

Women and solo travellers

Sri Lankan society is rather traditional in outlook, and the way you dress contributes greatly to people's opinion of you, and also to the way they behave towards you. Women and solo travellers should dress conservatively (at least away from established tourist beaches) and be firm, even rude, to unwarranted attention.

Unfortunately, solo travellers, whether male or female, especially on beaches, will attract attention from male opportunists who refuse to believe you really want to be left alone. To deter them, walk away and avoid conversation – and definitely eye contact – as this is seen as encouragement. On trains or buses, be wary of the male who sits beside you when there are plenty of seats elsewhere.

Be aware of warning signs

LANGUAGE

The fact that so many Sri Lankans speak good English means that very few foreigners – including many people who live on the island – make the effort to learn any Sinhala or Tamil. Sri Lankans are therefore very unused to hearing foreigners attempting to speak their native languages and so usually respond to most attempts to do so with a mixture of incomprehension and hilarity. It's worth persevering, however, and once your listeners have got over the initial shock, they will usually respond enthusiastically to your attempts to mangle and mispronounce their rather tongue-twisting language. Many Sinhalese nouns are a simple adaptation of English words with an added *-eka*. A bus is *buseka*, a torch is *torcheka*. When in doubt or put on the spot, simply try this rule – it actually goes a long way.

Sinhala

Greetings and phrases
Yes *Ow*
No *Naa*
Hello/good day *Ayubowan*
Thank you *Istuti*
Thank you very much *Bohoma istuti*
How are you? *Kohomadhe?*
Fine *Varadak neh*
Please *Karunakerara*
What is your name? *Nama mokadhdha?*
My name is.... *Mage nama....*

OK/very good *Hari hondai*
Delicious *Hari rasai*
I don't understand *Mata terinneh neh*
Very expensive *Hari ganan*
No sugar please *Seeni netuwa*
Please stop here *Metana nawaththanna*
Where are you going? *Koheda yanna?*
Where is the hotel? *Hootale kohedha?*
Where is the station? *Stesemeta eka ko?*
What is this? *Mekeh mokadeh?*
May I telephone? *Mata call ekak ganda poluwandeh?*
How much (is this)? *(Meeka) kiyadha?*
Do you speak English? *Ingirisi dannevada?*
I don't speak Sinhala *Singhala danna naa*

Questions
What? *Mokadhdha?*
When? *Kawadadha?*
Where? *Kohedha?*
Who? *Kaudha?*
Why? *Ayi?*

Days of the week
Monday *Sanduda*
Tuesday *Angahauwada*
Wednesday *Badada*
Thursday *Brahaspathinda*
Friday *Sikurada*
Saturday *Senesurada*
Sunday *Irida*

Sinhalese script   *It's always good to know a few phrases*

Place names

Many Sinhalese place names are long but quite logical as they are nearly always a compound, so remember a few rules and you will pronounce them like a native speaker.

island *duwa*
village *gama*
river *ganga*
street *mawatha*
road *para*
city *nuwara*
stream *oya*
town *pura*
port *tota, tara*
temple *vihara*
lake *weva*
bank *bank eka*
breakfast *udee tee*
clean *pirisidu*
coffee *kopi*
dinner *paa kaama*
dirty *kilutu*
food *kaama*
hotel *hotela*
lunch *dawal kaama*
small *punchi*
pharmacy *bet sappuwa*
restaurant *apana sala*
room *kaamare*
soap *saban*
tea *tey*
this/that *meke/oya*
water *watura*

Numbers
1 *eka*
2 *deka*
3 *tuna*
4 *hatara*
5 *paha*
6 *haya*
7 *hata*
8 *ata*
9 *namaya*
10 *daaha*
11 *ekolaha*
12 *dolaha*
13 *daha tuna*
20 *vissa*
30 *tiha*
40 *hataliha*
50 *panaha*
60 *heta*
70 *heddawa*
80 *assuwa*
90 *annuwa*
100 *seeiye*
1,000 *daha*

Social media
Are you on Facebook/Twitter? *Oba Facebook-eke hari/Twitter-eke hari inna-waada?*
What's your user name? *Obaghe user-name-eka kumakdha?*
I'll add you as a friend. *Mam-ma obawa yahaluwek vidhihata add-karannam.*
I'll follow you on Twitter. *Ma-ma obawa Twitter-eke follow-karannam.*
Are you following...? *Oba .....-wa follow karanawaada?*
I'll put the pictures on Facebook/Twitter. *Mam-ma Facebook-eke/Twitter-eke pictures-dhannam.*

A local on Negombo beach

I'll tag you in the pictures. *Mam-ma oyaawa pictures-wala tag-karannam.*

Tamil

Basics
Hello *Vanakkam*
Goodbye *Poyvituvarukiren* (Reply *Poyvituvarungal*)
Yes *Amam*
No *Illai*
Perhaps *Oruvelai*
Thank you *Nandri*
How are you? *Celakkiyama?*
What is your name? *Ungal peyar yenna?*
My name is (John/Jane) *Yen peyar (John/Jane)*
Where is the (hotel)? *(Hotel) yenge?*
What is this/that? *Idu/Adu yenna?*
What is the price? *Yenna vilai?*
That is very expensive *Anda vilai mikavum adikum*
I want (coffee) *(Kapi) Vendum*
I like (dosa) *(Dosai) Pudikkum*
Is it possible? *Mudiyuma?*
I don't understand *Puriyadu*
Enough *Podum*

Useful words
Toilet *Tailet*
Train *Rayil*
Bed *Kattil*
Room *Arai*
Bedroom *Patukkai arai*
Sari *Pudavai*
Dhoti *Vesti*
Towel *Tundu*
Sandals *Ceruppu*
Money *Punam*
Temple *Kovil*

Verbs
Come! (imperative) *Varungal*
Go (imperative) *Pongal*
Stop (imperative) *Nillungal*
Sleep *Tungu*
Eat *Sappidu*
Drink *Kudi*
Buy *Vangu*
Pay (money) *Punam kodu* (literally 'give money')
See *Par*
Wash (clothes) *Tuvai*
Wash (yourself) *Kazhavu*

Questions
How? *Yeppadi?*
What? *Yenna?*
Who? *Yar?*
Why? *Yen?*
Where? *Yenge?*
When? *Yeppodu?*
How much? *Yettanai/Yevvalavu?*

Days of the week
Monday *Tingal*
Tuesday *Cevvay*
Wednesday *Putam*
Thursday *Viyazhan*
Friday *Velli*
Saturday *Ceni*
Sunday *Nayiri*
Today *Inraikku*
Week *Varam*
Month *Matam*
Year *Varutam*

Many signs are also in English   *Universal language*

Numbers
1 *onru*
2 *irandu*
3 *munru*
4 *nanku*
5 *aindu*
6 *aru*
7 *yezhu*
8 *yettu*
9 *onpadu*
10 *pattu*
11 *patinonru*
12 *pannirandu*
20 *irupadu*
30 *muppadu*
40 *rarpadu*
50 *aimpadu*
60 *arupadu*
70 *alupadu*
80 *yenpadu*
90 *tonnuru*
100 *nuru*
100,000 *latcam*
10,000,000 *kodi*

Health
I am sick (vomiting) *Utampu cariyillai irukkiradu*
I have a pain *Vali irukkiradu*
I have diarrhoea *irrukkiradu*
Doctor *Taktar*
Help! *Utavi cey!*

Food
Food *Sappadu*
Water *Tunnir*
Rice *Sadum*
Fruit *Puzham*

Vegetables *Kaykuri*
Milk *Pal*
Coconut *Tengay*
Mango *Mampazham*
Banana *Valaippazham*
Coffee *Kapi*
Tea *Ti*
Steamed rice cakes *Idli*
Pancake made from fermented dough *Dosai*
Thin, spicy soup, usually with a tamarind base *Vadai Rasam*
Dry vegetable curry *Poriyal*
Chicken curry *Kolikarri*
Lamb curry *Attukkari*
Sweet festival dish *Payasam*
Mils 'Meals', similar to a North Indian thali (a selection of different small dishes), traditionally served on a banana leaf

Social media
Are you on Facebook/Twitter? *Neenga Facebook-il allathu/Twitter-il irrukireerkala?*
What's your user name? *Ungal paeyanar payar enna?*
I'll add you as a friend. *Naan ungalai nanbaraaha saerkiraen.*
I'll follow you on Twitter. *Naan ungalai twitter-il pinpatuvaen.*
Are you following...? *Neengal...ai pinpatureerkalaa?*
I'll put the pictures on Facebook/Twitter. *Naan Facebook-il/Twitter-il padangalai pordhukiraen.*
I'll tag you in the pictures. *Naan padangalil ungalai tag-panuvaen.*

Sri Lankan author Michael Ondaatje

BOOKS AND FILM

With its fascinating history and recent political tumult, Sri Lanka has inspired many authors of fiction, non-fiction and various specialist areas ranging from architecture to bird-watching. The below list suggests the best background reading to discover more about this diverse and dramatic country. There is a small but strong Sinhala-language film industry producing films for local cinemas (*Sulanga Enu Pinisa* and *Purahanda Kaluwara* are two of the best known), but some more-internationally famed movies have taken advantage of the country's lush scenery and been shot here too.

Books

Fiction
Colpetty People Ashok Ferrey. Entertaining vignettes, full of comedy and social insights, by one of Sri Lanka's leading short story writers.
Funny Boy Shyam Selvadurai. Touching novel chronicling the life of a young Tamil boy growing up in Colombo in the years leading up to the civil war.
The Hamilton Case Michelle de Kretser. Cleverly plotted and beautifully written whodunnit set in the British colonial era and chronicling the life and career of lawyer Sam Obeysekere and his chance involvement in the murder of a British planter.

The Jam Fruit Tree trilogy Carl Muller. This popular trilogy of novels (*The Jam Fruit Tree*, *Yakada Yaka* and *Once Upon A Tender Time*) describes the comic misadventures of the slow-witted Von Bloss family, lower-class railway Burghers living in Colombo and Kandy.
Reef Romesh Gunesekera. Shortlisted for the Booker Prize, this strangely captivating novel describes the relationship between Sri Lankan marine biologist Mister Salgado and his young houseboy cook Triton, giving a distinctive flavour of the island's cooking and history.
Running in the Family Michael Ondaatje. This superbly written memoir describes the maverick lives, loves and extended bouts of drunkeness of Ondaajte's Sri Lankan Burgher relatives, beautifully capturing the eccentric flavour of a vanished era. Ondaatje's other Sri Lankan book, the novel *Anil's Ghost*, is altogether darker, offering a lightly fictionalised account of the island during the civil war and JVP insurrection.
The Village in the Jungle Leonard Woolf. Superbly depressing tale of life in the backwaters of southern Sri Lanka – a place Woolf knew intimately from his work as a colonial administrator in Hambantota.

History and travel
Colombo Carl Muller. Readable, lightly fictionalised look into the history and

Alec Guinness in 'The Bridge on the River Kwai'

dark underbelly of the nation's capital city – and perhaps explaining why Muller himself chooses to live in Kandy.

A History of Sri Lanka K.M. de Silva. The best history of Sri Lanka, presenting an intelligent overview of the island's political and cultural history.

Only Man Is Vile William McGowan. Superbly insightful and disquieting account of war-torn Sri Lanka in the late 1980s during its twin struggles against the Tamil Tigers and JVP.

Reaping the Whirlwind K.M. de Silva. Classic account of the political background and ethnic conflict underpinning the island's long-running civil war.

Tea Time with Terrorists: A Motorcycle Journey into the Heart of Sri Lanka's Civil War Mark Stephen Meadows. Insightful account of a journey through the war zones of northern Sri Lanka and the various characters encountered en route.

A Year in Green Tea and Tuk-tuks Rory Spowers. Entertaining and thought-provoking account of a British environmentalist's attempts to create a sustainable eco-farm in the hills above Galle.

Art and architecture

The Architecture of an Island Barbara Sansoni, Ronald Lewcock and Laki Senanayake. Beautiful line drawings and descriptions of 95 classic Sri Lankan structures, from chicken coops to colonial cathedrals.

Geoffrey Bawa: The Complete Works David Robson. Sumptuous volume covering the work of Sri Lanka's foremost modern architect, with insightful text and superb photography.

Specialist guides

A Field Guide to the Birds of Sri Lanka John Harrison and Tim Worfolk. The definitive field handbook to the island's immense ornithological riches.

A Photographic Guide to the Birds of Sri Lanka Gehan de Silva Wijeyeratne et al. Excellent little pocket guide with good photographs of all Sri Lankan bird species along with useful accompanying notes.

Film

The Bridge on the River Kwai (1957). Classic war film depicting the construction of the Burma Railway in 1942–43 and starring William Holden and Alec Guinness, which was filmed in what was then Ceylon. The bridge in the film was located near Kitulgala.

Indiana Jones and the Temple of Doom (1984). This second in the blockbusting franchise was partly shot on location around Kandy, after the Indian authorities refused permission to Steven Spielberg and co on the grounds of finding the material offensive to India and Hinduism.

A Common Man (2013). Sir Ben Kingsley stars in this remake of an Indian film about an anonymous man planting bombs throughout Colombo and using this threat as leverage to have four notorious terrorists released from prison.

ABOUT THIS BOOK

This *Explore Guide* has been produced by the editors of Insight Guides, whose books have set the standard for visual travel guides since 1970. With top-quality photography and authoritative recommendations, these guidebooks bring you the very best routes and itineraries in the world's most exciting destinations.

BEST ROUTES

The routes in the book provide something to suit all budgets, tastes and trip lengths. As well as covering the destination's many classic attractions, the itineraries track lesser-known sights. The routes embrace a range of interests, so whether you are an art fan, a gourmet, a history buff or have kids to entertain, you will find an option to suit.

We recommend reading the whole of a route before setting out. This should help you to familiarise yourself with it and enable you to plan where to stop for refreshments – options are shown in the 'Food and Drink' box at the end of each tour.

For our pick of the tours by theme, consult Recommended Routes for... (see pages 6–7).

INTRODUCTION

The routes are set in context by this introductory section, giving an overview of the destination to set the scene, plus background information on food and drink, shopping and more, while a succinct history timeline highlights the key events over the centuries.

DIRECTORY

Also supporting the routes is a Directory chapter, with a clearly organised A–Z

of practical information, our pick of where to stay while you are there and select restaurant listings; these eateries complement the more low-key cafés and restaurants that feature within the routes and are intended to offer a wider choice for evening dining. Also included here is a handy language guide and our recommendations for books and films about the destination.

ABOUT THE AUTHORS

This edition was updated by Malgorzata Anczewska, building on the work of writer Gavin Thomas. Gavin has been visiting Sri Lanka for well over a decade, travelling to every corner of the country and seeing at first hand the varying effects of civil war, tsunami and peacetime reconstruction. He has worked on numerous guidebooks to the island including *Insight Guide Sri Lanka*, as well as contributing to other Insight Guides including books on India, Dubai, the UAE and Oman. *Explore Sri Lanka* builds upon content originally created by Royston Ellis, who has lived in Sri Lanka for over 35 years.

CONTACT THE EDITORS

We hope you find this Explore Guide useful, interesting and a pleasure to read. If you have any questions or feedback on the text, pictures or maps, please do let us know. If you have noticed any errors or outdated facts, or have suggestions for places to include on the routes, we would be delighted to hear from you. Please drop us an email at hello@insightguides.com. Thanks!

CREDITS

Explore Sri Lanka
Editor: Sarah Clark
Author: Gavin Thomas, Malgorzata Anczewska
Head of Production: Rebeka Davies
Update Production: AM Services
Picture Editor: Tom Smyth
Cartography: original cartography Berndtson & Berndtson GmbH, updated by Carte
Photo credits: Alamy 62T, 64/65, 121; AWL Images 42/43; Bigstock 6BC, 19L; Casa Colombo 88; Chaaya Hotels & Resorts 97L; Cinnamon Hotels 100; Dreamstime 34, 60/61, 65L; Fotolia 56, 102; Getty Images 1, 4/5T, 8/9T, 10, 10/11T, 11T, 11M, 12, 13, 14, 14/15, 15L, 28/29T, 30, 31, 32, 35, 86/87T, 120; Hafiz Issadeen 44; Heritance Hotels 93L, 95L, 96, 102/103; Indi Samarajiva 8ML, 8MR, 22, 23T, 28MR, 36, 40, 41L, 62B, 63L, 62/63, , 110, 110/111, 115; iStockphoto 8MR, 17B, 33, 38, 39, 40/41, 53L, 74/75, 82, 83, 84, 101; Jetwing Hotels 16, 86MC, 89, 90, 91, 92, 92/93; Leonardo 94, 94/95, 96/97; Marcus Wilson Smith/ Apa Publications 103L; Mount Lavinia Hotel 98, 98/99, 99L; Noel Rodrigo/Leopard Safaris 85; Scala Archives 26; Sri Lanka Tourism 4ML, 6TL, 17T, 18, 18/19, 24, 24/25, 25L; SuperStock 64; Sylvaine Poitau/Apa Publications 4MC, 4MR, 4MC, 4ML, 6MC, 6ML, 7T, 7MR, 7M, 7MR, 8ML, 8MC, 8MC, 20, 20/21, 21L, 23B, 27, 28ML, 28MC, 28ML, 28MC, 28MR, 36/37, 37L, 45, 46, 47, 48, 49, 50, 50/51, 51L, 52, 52/53, 54, 55, 56/57, 57L, 58, 59, 66, 67, 68, 69L, 68/69, 70, 70/71, 71L, 72, 73, 74, 75L, 76, 77, 78, 79, 80, 80/81, 81L, 86ML, 86MC, 86MR, 86MR, 104, 105, 106, 106/107, 107L, 108, 109, 111L, 112/113, 114, 116, 116/117, 117L, 118, 119L, 118/119; Tintagel 86ML
Cover credits: Robert Harding (main Shutterstock (bottom)

Printed by CTPS – China
All Rights Reserved
© 2017 Apa Digital (CH) AG and Apa Publications (UK) Ltd

Second Edition 2017

No part of this book may be reproduced, stored in a retrieval system or transmitted in any form or means electronic, mechanical, photocopying, recording or otherwise, without prior written permission from Apa Publications.

Every effort has been made to provide accurate information in this publication, but changes are inevitable. The publisher cannot be responsible for any resulting loss, inconvenience or injury.

DISTRIBUTION

UK, Ireland and Europe
Apa Publications (UK) Ltd
sales@insightguides.com
United States and Canada
Ingram Publisher Services
ips@ingramcontent.com
Australia and New Zealand
Woodslane
info@woodslane.com.au
Southeast Asia
Apa Publications (Singapore) Pte
singaporeoffice@insightguides.com
Hong Kong, Taiwan and China
Apa Publications (HK) Ltd
hongkongoffice@insightguides.com
Worldwide
Apa Publications (UK) Ltd
sales@insightguides.com

SPECIAL SALES, CONTENT LICENSING AND COPUBLISHING

Insight Guides can be purchased in bulk quantities at discounted prices. We can create special editions, personalised jackets and corporate imprints tailored to your needs.
sales@insightguides.com
www.insightguides.biz

INDEX

MAP LEGEND

- ● Start of tour
- → Tour & route direction
- ❶ Recommended sight
- ❷ Recommended restaurant/café
- ★ Place of interest
- ❶ Tourist information
- ♟ Statue/monument
- ♟ ψ Buddhist/Hindu temple
- ⊠ Main post office
- 🚌 Main bus station
- ∴ Ancient Site
- - - - - Ferry route
- ▬ ▬ National park boundry
- ▬▬▬ Province boundary
- - ▬ ▬ District boundary
- ☐ Park
- ☐ Important building
- ☐ Hotel
- ☐ Transport hub
- ☐ Shopping / market
- ☐ Pedestrian area
- ☐ Urban area
- ☐ Marsh